HOW TO WIN CASH, CARS, TRIPS & MORE!

Carolyn Wilman
THE CONTEST QUEEN

7290268 Canada Inc.
(416) 356-1116
info@contestqueen.com

For details on quantity orders, contact the publisher at
orders@contestqueen.com

Paperback ISBN: 978-0-9939254-0-5
eBook ISBN: 978-0-9939254-1-2

Cover design by Mark Lobo of doze!gfx.

DEDICATION

To all the friends I have made on this amazing adventure I call contesting, and to the best contest buddy I could ask for, my daughter Nicole.

In memoriam:

Helene Hadsell
author of Contesting: The Name It & Claim It Game
June 1, 1924—October 30, 2010

Bob Mennell
contributor to You Can't Win If You Don't Enter
March 5, 1934—December 12, 2013

Dortha Schaefer
original member of The Affadaisies
November 21, 1920—January 23, 2013

TESTIMONIALS

The Contest Queen Has Taught Others How to Win Over $1 Million in Prizes!

Wendy Won a House

"I just wanted to follow-up on my email to you. You may remember I qualified on the radio with two local radio stations for a chance to win a house. 700 contestants, over approximately four months qualified for a chance to turn a key to see if it opened the front door. On May 8th, we attended the Gala Party, where upon entry you deposited your ballot with the assigned number into a drum. Throughout the evening there were thirty numbers selected. Mine came up in the second to last group of five. All thirty of us came to stage where thirty actual keys were in a fish bowl. You would pick a key from the bowl and try to open the door. Twenty-one people before me were unsuccessful. I chose the key that opened the door to a $250.000.00 home.

Two days prior to this event you sent me the link to Helene Hadsell, I listened … I SELECTED, PROJECTED, EXPECTED and COLLECTED. Is it a coincidence? This is my biggest win so far. Like the words in Elton Johns' song SOMEONE SAVED MY LIFE TONIGHT. I am on disability and with my husband out of work, we just had signed the papers to re-mortgage our current home to pay off debts. We were able to cancel the re-mortgage because of this wonderful event, and that is my story. THANK YOU!"
—Wendy in Barrie, ON

Full Story: http://bit.ly/WinaHouse

Delaney Won a Ferrari

"I want to thank Carolyn Wilman (or @ContestQueen on Twitter) as she has a great website, Contest Queen. It's sort of because of her that I started entering sweeps as well as blog giveaways because she has won quite a few and she has tips on bettering your odds. Well, dang if she wasn't right!"
—Delaney in Wichita, K

Full Story: http://bit.ly/WinaFerrari

Nicole Won a Car

"I was reading your newsletter on Monday, May 7th and I took note and wrote down on a sticky your saying "I am Lucky, I am a Winner, I am a Grand Prize Magnet". I placed it beside my computer to bring luck. I also got your book for a Christmas gift.

Around 6:30 p.m. that night, I got THE call and it was Angela from Treehouse TV. I was so excited since I was a potential winner of the grand prize - A Pontiac Montana SV6 loaded with toys! So amazing it's a $30,000 prize!! I wanted to put the phone down and start screaming but my husband kept on trying to calm me down.

I am going to Pontiac Mills in Oshawa this Saturday and they are going to do a presentation at 11:00 a.m. with Dora and Sponge Bob present for this event. Thanks Carolyn!"
—Nicole in Chelmsford, ON

Carolyn is a Winner!

"I attended the seminar and it was simply amazing. I had no idea how much information one could learn. You really do need an entire day to go through so many aspects including how winning contests can liven up your life and take you on many new adventures! I learned so much about the tools one can use today. There is a community of "contestors" who are enthusiastic and always having fun. The seminar was only 2 weeks ago and today I won my 1st contest!"
—Carolyn in Ottawa, ON

Sandra & Michael won a Trip to Outer Space

"We won $80,000! Yes, that's not a typo. We won the grand prize from the Proctor and Gamble Gillette Hitch a Ride to Outer Space Contest. We had the choice of a flight to outer space including the 3-4 days of training in Virginia to be weightless for 3-4 minutes or the cash. We took the cash!!

We scrambled to get the forms signed and sent (including a medical). A couple months later we got the cheque in the mail. WOW! We paid down our mortgage, bought a car and are having our bathroom renovated as we speak.

Thanks for all your help. I bought your book and have done pretty much everything you wrote about. I entered my name and my husband in the "single" contests and his name came up. I enter contests daily and your book has helped me organize things so well. I share my knowledge with anyone who wants to know. Being a stay at home mom and loving the Internet, it's

the best hobby out there - totally free and totally fun, don't you think? It's like Christmas every time I win. Who knows what will be next?!"
—Sandra & Michael in Thorndale, ON

TABLE OF CONTENTS

FOREWORD

I've always been a fan of riddles and logic puzzles. Here's one for you: What do a Rolling Stones concert in Berlin, a year's supply of ice cream, an electric guitar, a Caribbean cruise, a Diet Coke commercial, throwing the first pitch at an LA Dodgers game, a big screen television and cash from TV's "Wheel of Fortune" all have in common? Any guesses? Well, they're just a few of the more than 500 prizes I have won by entering sweepstakes and contests, which ultimately led to the media crowning me "The Sweepstakes King."

I know you're hungry to be a winner of sweepstakes and contests since you picked up this new edition from Carolyn Wilman, The Contest Queen. Let's get right to it, without delay! Here's the winning recipe to winning and I mean winning Big! Drum roll, please! Take equal parts of The Sweepstakes King and The Contest Queen, mix in a dash of persistence and patience, stir until well blended. And what do you get? The delicious, fulfilling and rewarding opportunity to increase your odds of winning cars, cash, vacations, TV's, computers and a limitless bevy of tasty prizes. Do you notice what's missing from this recipe? That would be luck, because, simply, no luck is required to be a consistent winner of sweepstakes and contests. Have I increased your appetite to be a winner? Well, Carolyn's new book will help you build a buffet of prizes that are sure to satisfy.

Before I became known as The Sweepstakes King, I was hooked on watching TV game shows. As a teenager, growing up in Florida, I fantasized that one day I'd be a real game show contestant and win a cavalcade of cash and prizes. After graduating from The University of Denver, I pounced on my childhood dream, drove to Hollywood and within a week I was selected to be a contestant on "Match Game," winning $6,000! Immediately, I wanted to audition for other game shows, but quickly learned of legal restrictions at the time, limiting individuals to only one game show appearance per year. At this point, I was already addicted to winning, so I immediately jumped in haphazardly entering numerous sweepstakes and contests. Sadly, despite my exhaustive efforts, I ended up empty handed and frustrated. Of course, I quickly attributed my lack of wins to not being lucky and basically threw in the towel.

Then, I took a breath and thought, maybe I could, through trial and error, devise a system for tipping the odds in my favor and actually start winning. Amazingly, things began to change rapidly. The first sweepstakes I applied my plan of attack resulted in me winning 3 color TV's, cash and an all-expense paid trip to the Caribbean, all from a single store promotion. From then on, it felt like the prize flood gates opened, and my rapid accumulation of prizes led to me writing my first how to book on winning.

I have shared my secrets for winning on many TV shows including ABC's "The View", CNN, The Howard Stern Show and "The Maury Povich Show." My latest best-selling book *How to Win Lotteries, Sweepstakes, and Contests, in the 21st Century* continues to educate and inspire people of all ages to join in the joy and excitement of this wonderful, rewarding hobby.

In addition to the prizes, entering sweepstakes and contests opens a wealth of experiences and friendships, including my collaboration with Carolyn Wilman. Over the years we have shared fun stories and have swapped winning ideas. I had a blast being a guest on her online radio show. Carolyn truly is The Queen of Contests and I'm honored that she is sharing some of my winning ways in her new book.

Other lasting friendships developed after winning a Diet Coke Caribbean cruise, which included winners from across America. Part of the prize was all of us starring in a commercial filmed aboard the cruise. Sometimes a souvenir from a win will stick with me for a long time, like the couple extra pounds I carry as a result of recently winning a year's supply of Ben and Jerry's ice cream.

I can't think of any other hobby that can potentially add riches to your life, while enriching your journey along the way. So, let it be known that the Sweepstakes King and the Contest Queen make a royal proclamation, for you to go forth, enter, have fun and win! Now you are well on the way to securing your own keys to the contest kingdom!

Steve Ledoux, aka The Sweepstakes King
Best-Selling Author of How to Win Lotteries, Sweepstakes, and Contests in the 21st Century

"Give luck a chance to happen."
Tom Kite

INTRODUCTION

I love entering contest and sweepstakes. I get such a thrill out of finding new ones and reading about all the different prizes that I could win, I get butterflies in my stomach. I daydream about all the various trips I could take, the cars I could drive, or what I would spend the cash on. I love getting notified I won a prize. I get all bubbly inside and I grin from ear to ear for hours. **I am passionate about sweeping.**

HOW WINNING CHANGED MY LIFE

I have good reason to feel this way. Sweeping has actually changed the course of my life. Winning prizes back in 1991 led to going on a trip to Barbados with my mom… and to the first date I had with my ex-husband, Craig.

It was early December 1990 and a popular Toronto radio station was broadcasting their morning show for a week in a large downtown department store window. I worked in a nearby office tower and every day I would stop by to watch and listen. One morning, they were giving away a prize pack that included tickets to the Ice Capades and a gift certificate for a trendy hair salon, to the first person that could show them a photo of children in their family; I whipped open my wallet and flashed the photo of my little cousins - winning the prize pack.

My mom had been home with the flu, so when I got home I gave her the gift certificate to the hair salon. We decided that when she felt better we would spend the day together; going to the salon, having lunch and Christmas shopping downtown.

The restaurant we had lunch at that day was giving away a trip to Barbados. As we left the restaurant, I realized I forgot to get the entry forms. I made Mom wait as I ran back inside. When I returned I told her I would fill the forms out later, since the restaurant was close to my office. I said, "If I win I'll take you and if you win you'll take me!"

On December 24th, we were all at home wrapping gifts in the living room when the phone rang. Mom went into the kitchen to answer the call. I could only hear her side of the conversation. The woman identified herself and stated my mom may have won a trip. Mom really doesn't like telemarketers and couldn't figure out what was going on, but since it was Christmas she decided not to hang up right away. The woman asked my mom; "Where is Barbados?" My Mom nearly said she didn't know. Instead, she said: "In the Caribbean." She was told she did in fact win the trip and the travel agency would contact her in January to make all the arrangements. My Mom was confused and asked, "How did I win this trip?" I heard that and screamed, "We won! We won!" The woman asked her, "Didn't you fill out a sweepstakes entry form?" My mom said, "I think one of my kids entered me," as I jumped up and down around her.

NOTE: In Canada, we are notified we are a "potential" winner and must correctly answer a Skill Testing Question before we are declared the "official" winner. (See chapter, You're a Winner!)

TIP: Remember to tell your friends and family when you have entered them in sweepstakes. This way they won't be caught off guard when they are contacted and inadvertently disqualify themselves.

We went the following April. It was really special to spend a whole week alone with my mom—we had the best time and we learned a lot about each other.

I always wanted to win another family trip so that my mom, my daughter and I could go together. November 2005 we won a trip for four to London, England. It was so much fun to go on another vacation with my mom, daughter and then-husband Craig!

TIP: If you wish to take children on the trip, read the rules and check out the destination's website to ensure children are allowed at the resort or hotel. It would be a shame to win a vacation for the family, only to discover that only you and your partner or a friend can go.

That's how I won the trip to Barbados, but I know some of you are wondering about that first date with Craig. Well, remember the four tickets to the Ice Capades I said I won? I gave away one set to a girlfriend in my office. Then I started inviting friends to see who would like to go with me. I must have invited thirty people—no one wanted to go. One day I was speaking to Craig, who at the time was a business acquaintance, and asked him to go with me. Unlike those thirty other people, he said yes. We had a great time. I thought I had made a new friend; he says it was our first date and I just didn't know it. Although we are no longer together, we had many wonderful adventures and will always be Nicole's parents.

Would we have begun a friendship that led to marriage and building our family had I not won those tickets? Who knows?

I continued to enter sweepstakes sporadically until I read an article that led me to become a "sweeper." (For complete definitions see the NOTE later in this chapter.)

At the time, I had been unemployed for the longest period I have ever experienced in my professional life. One night I was lying in bed, reading the August 2001 copy of Reader's Digest, when I came across an article called "Get in the Winner's Circle! Tips from a contest junkie who's proven that the best things in life are free" by Barb Taylor. I read and reread that article and as I did, I made a decision—from then on, I would win all the things I wanted in life; like a new car!

Get in the Winner's Circle!
Tips from a contest junkie who's proven that the best things in life are free
by Barb Taylor, from Calgary Herald

Vacations in Italy, Hawaii and Mexico. Doing rolls in a stunt plane or being whisked off in a limousine for a night of wining, dining and theatre. Hardly the lifestyle you'd expect for an average-income family of four living in a duplex and driving a rusty old Volvo. Certainly not the lifestyle we envisioned when I left my teaching job 12 years ago to become a stay-at-home mom.

Our magical life began in 1988 after a sleepless night spent attending to our newborn son. The following day I entered a contest sponsored by a local radio station, inviting listeners to send letters to Santa. I pleaded with Santa for one night of uninterrupted sleep. My entry was selected for a one-week trip to Lake Tahoe from radio station CJAY 92. I was hooked.

Now I enter lots of contests, anywhere from 200 to 300 a year. I find out about them while shopping for groceries, listening to the radio, browsing through magazines and regularly perusing a contest newsletter to which I subscribe. Over the years, I've spent three to four hours a week researching new contests and filling out forms.

But the hard work has paid off. I averaged $10,000 in annual winnings; I've won two Dirt Devils through the Safeway Score & Win; and I've gone on a total of 14 major trips thanks to this winning hobby. My writing talents have won me a fair share of prizes as well, everything from a pair of $1,000 earrings for a local magazine's limerick contest to a pair of lift tickets for a Calgary Herald-sponsored Ski Memories contest.

Our winnings have also included clothing, appliances, a backyard barbecue and a patio set. We rarely pay to go to a movie or theatrical production. We frequently dine on gift certificates we have won. The luxuries our income doesn't provide for, my contesting does. Even our children get in on the act and have won a bike, a skateboard and passes to local attractions.

We've watched beautiful sunsets in Maui (courtesy of the Lite 96 jet) and Oahu (thanks to KissFM), walked the Freedom Trail in Boston (Calgary Co-op supermarket and Kraft foods), and even sent my in-laws to Scotland (a cross-Canada random draw from United Distillers). Will it ever end? Not as long as I can fill out an entry for or clip a Universal Product Code, or UPC as it's known (the bar code on products you buy).

Most of the trips I have won fall into the middle "good-and besides it's free" category. While not all-inclusive, your major costs of airfare and accommodation are covered. You stay in above average accommodation, usually a three-star hotel. You are generally responsible for your own meals, spending money and, occasionally, airport taxes. Trips we've won in this category included a one-week trip to San José del Cabo at the tip of Mexico's Baja peninsula. We enjoyed beautiful, uncrowded beaches, drinkable water, and simple but clean accommodations.

My husband and I experienced our "dream come true" trip courtesy of a local real-estate developer. By dropping off three entry forms at a tour of show homes, we won a one-week trip to Florence, which included stopovers in Paris and London. In Florence, we stayed at the Hotel Brunelleschi in a $650-a-night room that had floor-to-ceiling louvered windows opening onto a tiny flowered courtyard. We had a breathtaking view of the Duomo and the Campanile.

Nowadays, friends often rub my arm for luck before they head off to buy their lottery tickets. I can only shake my head in wonder—I've never won anything in a lottery.

So, you must be wondering, how do I do it? In the world of contesting, luck really has nothing to do with it: it all comes down to effort and persistence. For every contest I win, there are a 100 I've lost. Here are some suggestions to put the odds in your favor:

DO

☑ Pick free contests. These are usually drawbox contests and can be found in grocery stores and other businesses. Radio and television phone-in contests also cost nothing to enter.

☑ Also, pick the "better odds" contest: Look for contests that have a limited contesting area, offer lots of prizes, require you to "do something" (write a story, solve a puzzle), or that run for a short time span.

☑ Enter often. If it's a "better odds" contest, I'll enter five to 20 times. Try to space your entry mailings throughout the length of the contest's running.

☑ Collect UPCs. Remember that hand-drawn facsimiles are usually accepted in mail-in contests, and believe me, they really work. I've won many contests using hand-drawn facsimiles.

☑ Subscribe to a newsletter detailing currently running contests. A good one is the Canadian Contest Newsletter, P.O. Box 776, Stn. U, Etobicoke, Ont. M8Z 5P9*. On the web, you can find them at: www.canadian.contests.com.

DON'T

☒ Don't swipe the entry pads and then stuff the draw box. Getting greedy may get you disqualified for taking unfair advantage.

☒ Don't try to win more than once a month on a given radio station. If you make a nuisance of yourself by trying to win every prize offered, you lower your chances of winning something you really want.

☒ Don't waste money sending in dozens, or hundreds, of entries to a contest that gives away only one prize. This is a quick road to contest burnout.

☒ Don't get scammed! If you've won a contest you haven't entered—beware! If you have to be earning $40,000 a year and are required to attend a sales presentation—think twice!

☒ Don't send money to receive a prize—EVER.
Reprinted with permission from the August 2001 Reader's Digest Canada.

*The website address and mailing address listed in the article for the Canadian Contests Newsletter have since changed to:

www.canadiancontests.com

Canadian Contests Newsletter
P.O. Box 23066, RPO McGillivray
Winnipeg, MB R3T 5S3

NOTE: See section, Newsletters, to find Canadian and American equivalent contest and sweepstakes newsletters you can subscribe to.

I began my sweeping hobby by surfing the web and discovering an entire community of people who enjoy entering and winning. I joined a few groups, signed up for a couple of newsletters and through trial and error came up with an Internet-based sweepstakes entering system that really works. How do I know my system works? My results, of course—I consistently win 5-15+ sweeps every month, month after month, year after year. I even had a month where I won 83 prizes!

I am so passionate about sweeping and excited about winning, I decided to write this book after the 100th person asked me what is my secret to winning so much. I knew I was onto something with the system I have developed over the past few years and I wanted to share my discoveries, ideas, thoughts and enthusiasm with others.

Then someone asked me, "Why would you give all your secrets away? Wouldn't teaching others how to be successful sweepers decrease your odds of winning?" It was a tough question...

I was contemplating whether or not I should continue to write the book while driving to a friend's house. On the way I passed a church. The service announcement board out front said "You Can't Lose Helping Others Win."

That clinched it—I thought, "That message is for me! God is telling me it is OK to write the book!" (I really wish I had taken a picture of the sign.)

In this book, I will cover everything from how I began, the ins and outs of the five ways to enter sweepstakes, the Online Winning System I have developed over years of entering (and entering and entering...), stories from fellow sweepers, and what pitfalls to avoid along with many tips and tricks to increase your odds of winning.

In the past, most books on the hobby of sweeping focused on only three methods of entering; in-person, phone-in and mail-in. This left out the field of Internet, and mobile phone contests, both of which are the fastest growing, and easiest way to enter sweepstakes available today. This book focuses on the online method of entering sweepstakes, with an extra focus on social media giveaways; Facebook, Twitter, Pinterest and Instagram. When I began entering sweepstakes on a daily basis there was no single source of sweepstaking information in Canada. My goal is to make this book (and the online resources on my website—*www.contestqueen.com*) a hub of all the sweepstaking resources available today in North America. With all this information at your fingertips, you can choose which methods of entry you want to participate in, which groups and forums you may want to join, and what types of sweepstakes you want to enter.

I feel sweeping is one of the best, most rewarding hobbies around and I am sure you will feel the same way after your first win. By reading this book and using the many ideas, tips and tricks included within, you may enjoy the hobby of sweeping as much as I do.

NOTE: Occasionally I use the word contestor in this book. In Canada we use the word contest interchangeably with the word sweepstakes or giveaway even though by definition they are different. (See section, Promotion Types.)

> **con·testor** (kŏn′tĕst′ər)
> n.   1. One who enters contests, sweepstakes, competitions, lotteries and raffles.

NOTE: You may have noticed that I have spelled the word contestor with an OR as opposed to an ER. There is a reason for this. I created the word contestor because the proper definition of a contester is someone who is protesting or disputing something. We're trying to win cars and big-screen TVs here, not contest a will!

> **con·testing** (kŏn′tĕst′)
> v.   1. The act of entering contests.

> **con·test** (kŏn′tĕst′)

n.   1. A struggle for superiority or victory between rivals.
       2. A competition, especially one in which entrants perform separately and are rated by judges. See Synonyms at <u>conflict</u>.

con·test·ed, con·test·ing, con·tests (kən′tĕst′) (kŏn′tĕst′)

v. tr. 1. To compete or strive for.
       2. To call into question and take an active stand against; dispute or challenge: **contest a will.** See Synonyms at <u>oppose</u>.

v. intr. 1. To struggle or compete; contend: **contested with** other bidders for the antique.

Probably from French conteste, from contester, to dispute, from Old French, to call to witness, from Latin contestari : com-, com- + testis, witness; see trei —in Appendix I.

con·test′a·ble adj.

con′tes·ta′tion (kŏn′tĕ-stā′shən) n.

con·test′er n.

con·tes·tant (kən-tĕs′tənt, kŏn′tĕs′tənt)
n.   1. One taking part in a contest; a competitor.
       2. One that contests or disputes something, such as an election or a will.

Copyright © 2011 by Houghton Mifflin Harcourt Publishing Company. Adapted and reproduced by permission from *The American Heritage Dictionary of the English Language, Fifth Edition.*

sweep·staker (sweep/stāk/ər)
n.   1. One who enters sweepstakes, contests, competitions, lotteries, and raffles in order to win prizes.

sweeper (sweep/ər)
slang for sweepstaker
n.   1. One who enters sweepstakes, contests, competitions, lotteries, and raffles in order to win prizes.

sweeping (sweep/ŋ)
v.   1. The act of entering sweepstakes.

What is an enthusiastic sweeper called? I have been called a professional sweeper. The term makes me uncomfortable because a professional is an expert in a specific field and is usually well paid for their skill and knowledge. I consider contesting to be a hobby because 1) it is not my occupation, 2) I do it for pleasure, and 3) I certainly could not live off my winnings.

Profession or Hobby?

pro·fes·sion·al (prə-fĕsh′ə-nəl)

adj.
1. a. Of, relating to, engaged in, or suitable for a profession: lawyers, doctors, and other professional people.
   b. Conforming to the standards of a profession: professional behavior.
2. Engaging in a given activity as a source of livelihood or as a career: a professional writer.
3. Performed by persons receiving pay: professional football.
4. Having or showing great skill; expert: a professional repair job.

n.
1. A person following a profession, especially a learned profession.
2. One who earns a living in a given or implied occupation: hired a professional to decorate the house.
3. A skilled practitioner; an expert.

hob·by (hŏb′ē)

n. pl. **hob·bies** An activity or interest pursued outside one's regular occupation and engaged in primarily for pleasure.

Copyright © 2011 by Houghton Mifflin Harcourt Publishing Company. Adapted and reproduced by permission from *The American Heritage Dictionary of the English Language, Fifth Edition.*

There are several terms used globally to describe someone who enters sweepstakes on a regular basis. In Canada we refer to ourselves as contestors because we enter contests. In the United States you refer to yourselves as sweepers because you enter sweepstakes. (If we did that in Canada, people would think we were curlers!) In the United Kingdom and Australia they refer to themselves as competitors because they enter competitions. As Shakespeare said, "A rose by any other name would smell as sweet." My favorite term to describe my hobby is *winner*!

The Winning Streak That Started it All

On a very cold gray day in January, I got the email that every contestor waits for: Congratulations! Your name has been drawn for the **Grand Prize**, Trip for two to L.A. and dinner with/prepared by Bob Blumer, in **Meyer's "The Surreal Meal" contest**, sponsored by Alliance Atlantis Broadcasting Inc. and Meyer Canada Inc. (Along with the trip to Los Angeles, I received an eight piece set of Meyer Anolon cookware and $500 spending money.)

TIP: You can collect frequent flyer points on the flights you have won. Each person must have their own account to maximize the free rewards on top of a win.

Craig and I arranged to take the trip in March. We arrived at the airport on Thursday morning and met our chaperone from Alliance Atlantis. (They need to ensure that their show's hosts are protected from crazy contestors.) It had been a slow month and I had not won a single thing. We got to L.A. and discovered we had two phone messages; one from my Dad and one from my stepmother. Due to the time difference I could not call until Friday morning. When I called, my stepmother said "Are you sitting down?" I was expecting bad news. She then proceeded to tell me my niece won a trip for four to New York City!

At the beginning of the year I told my stepsister, I was going to start entering my niece and nephew in sweepstakes for children. I thought they would enjoy receiving a neat new toy or DVD in the mail. Little did I know their first win would be "a big one!" (I consider it my win even though I didn't get the prize because I did the entering.) I was so happy for them since they had never been on a family vacation and they were now going on the trip of a lifetime.

We then proceeded to have an amazing time in Los Angeles. We arrived at Bob's home in the Hollywood Hills at 8:00pm on Friday evening. He had called me a few weeks before the trip to discuss the menu. We agreed he would make us recipes from his upcoming cookbook Surreal Gourmet Bites: show-stoppers and conversation starters. Bob is also an oenophile so each course was paired with a selection from his extensive private wine collection. He is a wonderful host. Craig and I felt as if we had gone to a friend's home for dinner. I went out and purchased his new book when it was released so I could continue to enjoy his creations and share them with my family and friends.

NOTE: There are no photos of our evening with Bob Blumer in this book. It is important to read all the documents you sign with regards to a sweepstakes win. The sweepstakes prize waiver (also referred to an affidavit or release form) stated all photos taken during our evening are for personal use only and cannot be published.

RECOMMENDED READING: Surreal Gourmet Bites: show-stoppers and conversation starters by Bob Blumer.

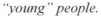

We arrived home late Sunday night, tired, happy and feeling lucky that we had such a memorable long weekend. As a contestor you never know how long a dry spell will last or how long a winning streak will continue. At 10:00am Monday morning Craig got a phone call from a local radio station. He won a two-week European holiday—a nine country, fourteen day bus tour. He was shocked.

We went to Europe that September. The trip was with a tour company that specialized in youth groups 18-35. It was fast paced and had a party atmosphere. Being up late every night, getting up early every morning and running around a new city almost daily took its toll on me by the end of the vacation. I came home with a terrible cold, having sadly discovered I wasn't 21 anymore and couldn't keep up the pace I use to. No wonder they say 18-35! It's really tough on those of us over 35.

TIP: If one half of the couple is under 35 and the other is over, the older person can sign a waiver stating you understand the tour is designed for "young" people.

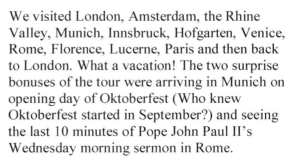

We visited London, Amsterdam, the Rhine Valley, Munich, Innsbruck, Hofgarten, Venice, Rome, Florence, Lucerne, Paris and then back to London. What a vacation! The two surprise bonuses of the tour were arriving in Munich on opening day of Oktoberfest (Who knew Oktoberfest started in September?) and seeing the last 10 minutes of Pope John Paul II's Wednesday morning sermon in Rome.

The highlight of the vacation for me was the evening trip up the Eiffel Tower. I have always wanted to go to Paris, and standing on the upper deck, hugging Craig and looking over the lights of Paris as the tower twinkled was absolutely magical. I felt so lucky!

Our best adventure on the tour was the morning we had a $100 breakfast. It was the second last day of the trip and we were in Paris. After a brief tour of a perfumery, we found ourselves outside of the Opera House. We were hungry and decided to have a bite to eat, and were tired of eating small, quick breakfasts. Looking around we noticed Le Café de la Paix, Paris' most famous restaurant. (Embarrassingly, I did not recognize the name. Craig did recognize the name, remembering many world famous chefs began their careers in that very café.) We entered from the street entrance and I was thinking we might sit outside. Craig and I discussed our eating options with the Maitre D', and decided we would like to have the breakfast buffet.

They sat us inside in a booth opposite the hotel entrance. As we waited for our tea and coffee to arrive we noticed several very well dressed people come into the restaurant.

Then we went to the buffet. I have never seen a buffet like this in my life! There were breads and cheeses from all over the world, twenty different kinds of fresh fruit, four types of fresh fruit juice, and the best scrambled eggs I have ever eaten. They even had an entire section of Japanese specialties. When I came back to the table I said to Craig, "I don't think we want to know what this breakfast is going to cost us." We sat for an hour relaxing, eating, and deciding what we were going to see that afternoon and soaking in the atmosphere. When the bill arrived it was €64 ($100). It was worth every penny!

Many people ask me when I have time to enter so many sweepstakes. I have to quote R.J. Ward from a sign we found in the Tinker Town Museum just outside Santa Fe, NM.

TIP: Before you begin entering sweepstakes that offer international travel as a prize, ensure all the people travelling with you have a valid passport and visas for some countries. Travel restrictions have become tighter over the past several years, so now many promotions state in the rules you must have a valid passport to enter.
United States http://bit.ly/USAPassport
Canada http://bit.ly/CanadaPassport

NOTE: All the web addresses, URLs, and other contact details listed in this book were correct at press time. The Internet is very fluid and URLs, websites, web page and emails change daily. I consistently post all changes and updates on my website at www.contestqueen.com.

WHY RUN A SWEEPSTAKES?

One question I get asked frequently is, "Do companies really give away all those prizes? It must be a scam."

Yes, they really do give away those prizes.

No one runs a sweepstakes because they are feeling generous. Sweepstakes, contests and giveaways are a way for companies to attract or keep customers, pure and simple. They use our desire for the prize as a lure to get us to buy their products and services or expose ourselves to their advertising message. The advantage to the company is that the lure of the prize will keep customers' attention longer than other forms of advertising—we want what they are giving away, and are willing to endure their message or buy more of a product or service than we normally would to give ourselves a better chance of winning.

Companies build sweepstakes into their total marketing and advertising annual budget because sweepstakes are a fun way to get a consumer involved with their product or service. In 2012, companies in the U.S. spent over $3 billion running sweepstakes. There are a lot of legitimate prizes to be won!

Companies run sweepstakes for a variety of specific reasons. They hold sweepstakes to:

- attract attention to their brand, product or service;
- increase sales;
- maintain or increase customer loyalty;
- increase their customer database;
- begin permission marketing. (You say it's OK for them to send you something via email or mail.)

NOTE: Any company that emails Canadians must ensure they are CASL (Canada Anti Spam Legislation) compliant meaning you are giving them expressed consent that it is OK to for the organization to contact you. http://bit.ly/FightSpam

A company needs to determine what it wants to accomplish and design a simple sweepstakes around that purpose.

If you ever feel a sweepstakes is confusing, complicated or unfair, contact the company promoting the sweepstakes (the judging agency or sweepstakes management company, the sponsor, or both) and ask for clarification of what you are finding frustrating.

Although technically illegal, I have seen companies change the entry page or the rules mid-promotion period, based on contestant feedback. Unfortunately, some companies make sweepstakes so complicated the original purpose of running the promotion is defeated.

STORY: Susan submitted a good story on how some companies miss the point of a promotion (to create product or service awareness and attract new customers) by making the sweepstakes too confusing or difficult to enter.

୨୦ଓଓ

Susan—Rose Bay, NS

Several years ago they had a sweepstakes in the local paper and you also had to listen to the local radio station for the daily clue letter. This went on for several weeks and my sister and I faithfully got each letter. They didn't have any letters for the weekends. If you didn't hear the letter, you could go to the local mall and the letters would be posted at the lotto booth. (It's 30 minute drive away for me.) You also had to cut four parts of a computer picture out of the local weekly paper (one each week for four weeks) and paste them on to the entry form. My other sister wanted to enter too, so she went to friends and got their old papers, since she and my mother share the paper.

When the sweepstakes was over you had a week to put your entries in. It only took my sister and I a few hours to figure out the phrase, KNOWLEDGE PAYS, from the letters given. I took my mom's entry out with mine. My other two sisters took their entry forms in separately.

At the end of the sweepstakes my mom got a call that she had won the computer, printer, camera and scanner. When I went to take Mom to collect her prize, we ended up chatting with the girl in the lotto booth (where the letters were posted), and she said the sweepstakes must have been too complicated as there were only eight entries. Great odds!!

Needless to say, my nephew (who lives with my mom most of the time) was in Grade 5 at the time, and it didn't take him long to hook up the computer. I wasn't there to see his eyes light up but I know he was thrilled to be able to do his homework on the computer. My mom, who was 70, didn't know much about it but wouldn't sell it and it wasn't hooked up to the Internet. What a wonderful win!

ಬಂಡ

The premise of the promotion Susan participated in was to use multiple mass media vehicles and get people to participate. However, it was so difficult and cumbersome that most people were scared away or couldn't be bothered to enter resulting in only eight entries.

TIP: If a sweepstakes seems complicated, don't let it discourage you from entering. As Susan found, you might not have many other entries to compete against, which will increase your chances of winning.

PROMOTION TYPES

There is a difference between a lottery, a contest and a sweepstakes. It is important to understand the differences because it could determine what types of promotions you prefer to enter.

Lotteries and Sweepstakes Versus Contests

You're probably aware of the words "lotteries," "sweepstakes," and "contests," but you may not really understand how they differ from one another. This section will discuss their differences, as well and their relative advantages and disadvantages.

It's easier to define sweepstakes and contests by starting with their more familiar grandfather: the lottery. A lottery is any game that consists of three elements. These three elements are chance (luck), the entry fee (sometimes referred to as the "consideration"), and the prize. The first element—luck—is introduced by the very fact that you're competing against thousands of other people by predicting several numbers that will be chosen at random. The entry fee is generally the price of the ticket itself. Most lottery tickets cost one dollar and the prizes are usually money.

What differentiates a sweepstakes or contest from a lottery is that one of these three elements has been removed. In a sweepstakes, that element is the entry fee. In other words, the game is still a game of chance, and there are still prizes to be won (although not necessarily cash prizes), but you don't have to pay to enter.

Contests retain the entry fee but remove the luck as a determining factor. The entry fee is usually in the form of purchasing one or more of the company's products. For example, a contest often requires you to send in a proof of purchase or label. Obviously, you cannot obtain these items without buying the product. It doesn't matter whether you personally bought it or one of your friends purchased it. The luck is removed by adding an element of skill. Whereas sweepstakes are determined through random drawings, contests require the participants to perform in some way. A contest may ask you to write a song or create a rhythm, or explain why you use a product. A panel of judges determines which contestant has demonstrated the most skill.

People tend to believe contests are more legitimate because they're sometimes required to pay an entry fee. One reason companies like contests so much is that they are another way of generating affordable advertising. Not only does the contest itself increase consumer interest, but the company might end up with a catchy slogan or jingle for its product when the contest is over. This slogan might just be as good as one created by a professional marketing firm, and the prize given to the winner is likely to be less expensive than hiring such a firm.

How to Win Lotteries, Sweepstakes and Contests in the 21st Century by Steve Ledoux. Copyright ©2004 Santa Monica Press LLC. Used by permission of Santa Monica Press LLC, 800-784-9553, www.santamonicapress.com.

The laws that govern contests and sweepstakes in Canada and the United States are very similar with a few glaring differences.

In Canada there are provisions in the Criminal Code and the Competition Act to ensure they are not "illegal lotteries". (See chapter, The Official Rules.)

Sweepstakes, scratch and win games and other contests where prizes are awarded by chance are classified as "lotteries" by the *Criminal Code*. The common law defines a lottery as a scheme with the following three elements: a prize; and award by chance; and money or other consideration paid by participants. Lotteries have been illegal for several hundred years, unless they are government sponsored. In 1802, the English Gaming Act addressed the problem as follows:

Whereas evil disposed Persons do frequently resort to Publick Houses and other Places, to set up certain mischievous Games or Lotteries ... and to induce Servants, Children, unwary Persons, to play at the said Games; and thereby most fraudulently obtain

great Sums Money from Servants, Children, and Unwary Persons, to the great Impoverishment and utter Ruin of many Families ...
[5]

[5] *Gaming Act*, 1802 (U.K.), 42 Geo. III, c. 119.

This material has been sourced, with permission, from Chapter 8 of Pritchard, Vogt: *Advertising and Marketing Law in Canada, 4th Edition* (LexisNexis Canada Inc.) (2012)

Why there are Skill Testing Questions in Canada

At common law in Canada, as in the United States, in order to avoid having your contests classified as an illegal lottery, you have to remove either chance *or* consideration from your promotion. (You could also remove the prize or prizes, but that would probably defeat your purpose.)

There are two ways to deal with the question of chance. The most straightforward is to eliminate chance altogether by conducting a pure skill contest.

The other way to deal with the question of chance is by adding an element of skill to a random selection process. Hence the ubiquitous skill-testing question requirement. The most common skill question is a three- or four-part mathematical question. The question is often found on entry forms in a contest where many prizes will be awarded. In a contest with relatively few prizes the skill-testing question is typically administered by telephone, mail or e-mail.

The preference for mathematical question has two sources. First, it is the easiest solution to the contest promoter's dilemma: skill is required, but promoters do not want contestants to get the answer wrong. Second, there is a long line of old Canadian cases that hold that various non-mathematical feats – such as shooting a turkey from a distance of 50 yards – do not constitute sufficient "skill" to avoid the "illegal lottery" prohibition.

This material has been sourced, with permission, from Chapter 8 of Pritchard, Vogt: *Advertising and Marketing Law in Canada, 4th Edition* (LexisNexis Canada Inc.) (2012)

See chapter, You're a Winner for examples and further explanations of Skill-Testing Questions.

One of the legal provisions in both Canada and the U.S. is the requirement for a No Purchase Entry (NPE). The NPE can be met by requiring the contestant submit a UPC (Universal Product Code) or a short essay.

Purchase Requirement:

Section 206 of the *Criminal Code* prohibits purchase requirements for all "games of chance or mixed chance and skill" where the prizes consist of "goods, wares or merchandise". In all such cases, you must have a no-purchase means of entry. Usually, this is a hand-drawn facsimile of the entry form and/or of the UPC. You can also require a short (50-100 words) hand-written essay. No-purchase entries should be treated with "equal dignity", and you cannot require no-purchase entrants to inconvenience themselves in a major way or expend considerably more effort than "purchase" entrants.

You *can* generally have a purchase requirement in two situations:

(a) in a skill contest, *i.e.*, a contest where winners are determined solely on the basis of skill such as a photography or writing contest where neither the consideration to enter nor the prize is considered "security"; and

(b) where *none* of the contest prizes falls into the category of "goods, wares or merchandise". Exempt prizes include cash, services (such as a car lease or a health club membership) and trips.

The "security" issue is raised by the somewhat ambiguous language of section 206(1)(e) of the Criminal Code and the cases where this section was judicially considered. This provision prohibits a scheme whereby the winner would receive a larger amount of "valuable security" than the sum paid by reason of the participation of others. This is a broad prohibition, and the Supreme Court of Canada has held that it applies to contests of pure skill and even in situations where the prize was held in trust prior to the contest starting. It is generally advisable, therefore, in the presence of security to have a no-purchase form of entry to avoid the potential application of section 206(1)(e). Section 2 of the *Criminal Code* defines "valuable security" using very technical terms (those of you who are lawyers can read it at your leisure) but includes things like evidence of payment and documents of title to lands or goods.

This material has been sourced, with permission, from Chapter 8 of Pritchard, Vogt: *Advertising and Marketing Law in Canada, 4th Edition* **(LexisNexis Canada Inc.) (2012)**

Lotteries

I frequently get asked if I play the lottery and how can someone pick the winning numbers. The answers are: only when I feel lucky because I don't like spending money on gambling very often and if I could pick the winning numbers I wouldn't enter sweepstakes!

There are several different types of lotteries: jackpot draws (Powerball, 649), daily draws (Big 4, Pick 3), and instant games (scratch and win) for example.

Information regarding each state's or province's lotteries can be located at the following websites. The websites are quite comprehensive and have everything from winning numbers to Frequently Asked Questions regarding each lottery.

NOTE: If a state or province is not listed, they do not offer lotteries.

Arizona
www.arizonalottery.com

California
www.calottery.com

Colorado
www.coloradolottery.com

Connecticut
www.ctlottery.org

Delaware
http://www.delottery.com/

District of Columbia
www.dclottery.com

Florida
www.flalottery.com

Georgia
www.galottery.com

Idaho
www.idaholottery.com

Illinois
www.illinoislottery.com

Indiana
www.hoosierlottery.com

Iowa
www.ialottery.com

Kansas
www.kslottery.com

Kentucky
www.kylottery.com

Louisiana
www.louisianalottery.com

Maine
www.mainelottery.com

Maryland
www.mdlottery.com

Massachusetts
www.masslottery.com

Michigan
www.michiganlottery.com

Minnesota
www.mnlottery.com

Missouri
www.molottery.com

Montana
www.montanalottery.com

Nebraska
www.nelottery.com

New Hampshire
www.nhlottery.com

New Jersey
www.njlottery.net

New Mexico
www.nmlottery.com

New York
www.nylottery.org

North Carolina
www.nc-educationlottery.org

North Dakota
www.ndlottery.org

Ohio

www.ohiolottery.com

Oklahoma
www.lottery.ok.gov

Oregon
www.oregonlottery.org

Pennsylvania
www.palottery.state.pa.us

Rhode Island
www.rilot.com

South Carolina
www.sceducationlottery.com

South Dakota
www.sdlottery.org

Tennessee
www.tnlottery.com

Texas
www.txlottery.org

Vermont
www.vtlottery.com

Virginia
www.valottery.com

Washington
www.walottery.com

West Virginia
www.wvlottery.com

Wisconsin
www.wilottery.com

Multi-State Lottery Association (www.musl.com) is entirely owned and operated by the member lotteries offering the games.

The Western Canada Lottery Corporation manages the lotteries for Alberta, Saskatchewan and Manitoba with the Yukon, Northwest Territories and

Nunavut as associate members.
www.wclc.com

The British Columbia Lottery Corporation manages British Columbia
www.bclc.com

The Atlantic Lottery Corporation manages the lotteries for New Brunswick,
Nova Scotia, Prince Edward Island, Newfoundland and Labrador.
www.alc.ca

The Ontario Lottery and Gaming manages Ontario.
www.olg.ca

Loto-Quebec manages Quebec.
www.loto-quebec.com

Lottery Canada is a national lottery portal.
www.lotterycanada.com

North American Association of State and Provincial Lotteries
(www.naspl.org) is an organization whose purpose is to be a hub of
information for its members.

*RECOMMENDED READING: Author Steve Ledoux has two chapters in his
book How to Win Lotteries, Sweepstakes and contests in the 21ˢᵗ Century
dedicated to winning lottery prizes.*

*RESOURCE: Learn How to Increase Your Chances of Winning the Lottery
by Richard Lustig. www.winninglotterymethod.com*

My Free Lottery Pool

www.myfreelotterypool.com

The odds of winning the lottery can be pitiful and you could potentially
waste hundreds of dollars gambling. Dan Bader (aka Captain Dano) came up
with a solution to that problem in 2007 by creating a website called My Free
Lottery Pool.

How does it work? Each week Dan purchases dozens of real PowerBall and
MegaMillions lottery tickets paid for with advertising revenue generated
from the site's traffic. He posts an image of the actual tickets on the site
where members can view the tickets and register into the 100% Free Lottery
Pools. If any one of the free lottery tickets match the official drawing results,
everyone who is registered in the winning pool will share in the multi-million
dollar jackpot. No Spam. No Scam. No Gimmicks. Nothing to Buy. Simply
sign up and register. It's open to anyone 18 years or older worldwide.

My Free Lottery Pool is a Freemium site. Basic membership is free, but to cover additional operating costs, if you purchase a First Cabin shirt from his Cafe Press store you become a member of the First Cabin Club and get guaranteed, automatic pool entry into every lottery pool he opens.

Additional site features include: Daily Fortune Cookies and Inspirational Messages; Member Predictions; Worldwide Lottery News & Results; Free Alerts for Powerball, Megamillions and Super-Lotto Results; Casino and Word Games, and much more.

Be sure to subscribe to Dan's YouTube channel as he posts winning affirmations, focus numbers and other positive videos. (See section, Law of Attraction.)

Non-members who have purchased this book can also get a special prize when they subscribe by using the URL: www.myfreelotterypool.com/CQ.

RESOURCE: There are many legitimate online lottery sites, but there are many more lottery scams. Lotto Exposed is a site dedicated to exposing lottery frauds, scams and outright crooks. They also post interesting articles on the lottery in general. www.lottoexposed.com

Sweepstakes

The main focus of this book is sweepstakes. All the promotions I discuss, the methods of entry, and my Online Winning System are about sweepstakes. When I meet fellow contestors online or post to one of the sweepstaking discussion groups, it is usually about a sweepstakes. This is because sweepstakes, in general, require the least amount of effort to enter and can reap a great reward. You just need to fill out an entry form, submit it and hope you win. Most of the promotions I enter are sweepstakes. I enter a few contests and, on occasion, I buy lottery tickets.

Contests

There are all types of contests you can enter: cooking, baking, woodworking, writing and photography, to name just a few. These are great to enter because the number of entrants is usually quite low due to the extra "skill" work involved compared to sweepstakes (with the exception of the Annual Pillsbury Bake Off which garners thousands of entries). So, if you have a particular hobby, skill or talent, look for contests where you can, not only enjoy what you are doing (e.g. taking photographs, writing poetry or inventing new recipes), you can possibly also win cash and/or prizes doing it.

Ironically, I rarely enter essay and story-based contests. Let me explain. These types of contests are usually judged on the best story. I may write well, however, I feel I usually do not have a story good enough to win. I occasionally enter cooking and baking contests because cooking and baking are another love of mine. For example, my chili recipe won 3rd prize in a Super Bowl of Chili Cook Off in 2002.

Carolyn's Award-Winning Awesome Chicken Chili

3lbs. ground chicken (I prefer to grind my own using skinless boneless thighs.)
1 large Spanish onion, diced
1 tbsp. canola oil
4 large or 6 medium tomatoes, diced (a can of diced tomatoes can be used if desired)
1 green pepper, seeded and diced
1 red pepper, seeded and diced
1 yellow pepper, seeded and diced
1 orange pepper, seeded and diced
1 cubanelle pepper, seeded and diced
1 hot banana pepper, seeded and diced
1 jalapeno pepper, seeded and diced
1 chili pepper, seeded and finely diced (use gloves for this step, trust me!)
1 tbsp. chili powder*
1 tbsp. hot chili flakes*
10 dashes of Tabasco
1 tsp. salt*
1 tsp. ground black pepper*
1 19oz. can black beans, drained and rinsed
1 19oz. can kidney beans, drained and rinsed

This is one of the easiest recipes ever. I place all the ingredients (except for the oil, the onion and the chicken) in an 8qt. pot and turn the heat on low. In a cold frying pan pour in the oil and turn the heat on medium low (the cooking temperatures were determined by my halogen stove top and may be adjusted for your stove). Once the oil is hot, turn the heat to low, put the onion in the pan, sauté until soft, and then add the onion to the pot. In the same frying pan, place the raw chicken (add a bit more oil if it is required) and cook until there is no pink color left. (I find the chicken browns faster if I put the lid on the frying pan.) Drain the

35

> chicken and then add the chicken to the pot. Stir about every ½
> hour. Put the lid on until the chili boils then I find the chili turns
> out best if cooked on low without a lid for 3-4 hours. Otherwise,
> there is too much liquid and it is too runny to scoop with chips.
> *to taste

My prize for such a delicious recipe was a nice basket of Tabasco branded
goodies including an apron, a golf shirt, a silk scarf and enough Tabasco
sauce to make a ton of chili!

I also collect cookbooks. My father purchased an old box at an auction, in the
box was The Nellie Aldridge Cook Book—Many Ways to Utilize the Citrus
Fruits of the San Bernardo Valley. The book is undated. Inside is a wonderful
example of a contest entry from days gone-by.

> **Orange Sunshine Cake**
> Whites of 10 eggs, yolks of 6 eggs; 1 cup granulated sugar, 1
> teaspoon flavoring, 1 cup Swan's Down cake Flour, 1 teaspoon
> cream of tartar. Beat whites of eggs until stiff and dry, add sugar
> gradually and continue beating; then add yolks of eggs beaten
> until thick and lemon colored, and 1 teaspoon orange extract. Cut
> and fold in flour mixed and sifted with cream of tartar. Bake 60
> minutes in a slow oven*, in an angel cake pan.
>
> In a cake baking contest held by Misses Hancock and Wade of
> the Home Furniture Company of San Bernardino this cake scored
> 98½ points winning a $55.00 Acorn Gas Range, given as a prize
> for the best cake.
> *A slow oven is 300°F.

Be aware there is a difference between a contest that wants you to submit a
story (e.g. why your mom is the best) and a sweepstakes' no purchase entry
option asking you to submit your entry along with a 25-250 word essay. The
contest winner will be selected by a panel of judges and the sweepstakes
winner will be drawn at random. Therefore, even if you feel you don't have
the best creative writing skills, and wouldn't enter the contest, enter the
sweepstakes as your writing skills will not be judged.

*RECOMMENDED READING: How to Win Lotteries Sweepstakes and
Contests in the 21st Century (2nd Edition) by Steve Ledoux for Recipe
Contests and his Top 6 Entry Tips.*

Anybody can win unless there
happens to be a second entry."
George Ade

THE OFFICIAL RULES

My #1 tip:
Read The Official Rules
and Follow Them!

This is my number one tip because most people don't read the official rules. One company I interviewed said only 2% of the people clicked the Official Rules button on online sweepstakes entry pages. Another source stated that up to 40% of mail-in entries were disqualified because the official rules were not followed.

It is <u>very important</u> to read the Official Rules to see:

- the start and end dates of the sweepstakes;
- if you are eligible to enter;
- how many times you can enter;
- how many people in the household can enter;
- any other rules specific to that sweepstakes.

I have potentially disqualified myself countless times by not reading the rules before I enter. I have entered:

- out-of-state or out-of-country sweepstakes;
- more than once in a one-entry-per-person sweepstakes;
- both my spouse and myself in one-entry-per-household sweepstakes;
- before the sweepstakes starts;
- my spouse in women only sweepstakes;
- sweepstakes where I did not meet the age requirements.

Many sweepstakes have overlapping methods of entry. Reading the official rules will also allow you to determine the best entry method for you.

All sweepstakes must have official rules. The Official Rules is the contract between the sponsor of the sweepstakes and people that are eligible to enter. The official rules CANNOT change once the rules have been published and entries have been accepted.

The official rules typically contain the following information: 1) A statement that "No Purchase Necessary"; 2) entry period (start and end dates); 3) eligibility requirements (age, residency, also specify exclusions); 4) how to enter – including a "no purchase" method of entry (also known as an alternative method of entry); 5) any limitations on the number of entries which could be daily or for the entire entry period; 6) odds of winning; 7) description and retail value of the prizes; 8) how and when the winners will be selected and notified; 9) limitation or restrictions on the prize; and 10) Sponsor's name and address. Additional disclosures are required depending on the type of promotion and industry. Social media promotions may trigger other additional requirements.

Courtesy of Adam Solomon, Michelman & Robinson LLP, (212) 730-7700, www.mrllp.com

Each state has varying laws governing sweepstakes. Gambling lawyer Chuck Humphrey, of Gambling-Law-US, created a wonderful online resource of U.S. gambling laws. Visit www.gambling-law-us.com/State-Laws/. Click on each state to read the text of these laws, including the full text of any specific sweepstakes laws. (See section, Government Regulations.)

BEHIND THE SCENES: Adam Solomon of Michelman & Robinson LLP discusses sweepstakes from a lawyer's perspective.

၈ဝ၃

Adam Soloman—www.mrllp.com

Historically sweepstakes may have had more pre-planning, longer business cycle, better logistics and operation. Today with things moving at the speed of social media some promotions are run "off the cuff". This change of pace and lack of attention to detail can have serious legal implications.

Sweepstakes sponsors or agencies cannot forget that the official rules are required and is the contract between the sponsor and the entrant. Rushing a promotion and not ensuring the promotion is properly structured or a well drafted rules is in place, means there could be problems for all parties involved. Even though technologies have changed, the laws governing sweepstakes have no. All promotions, regardless of execution, should ensure they comply with current sweepstakes laws.

Promotional lawyers should be called in at the beginning of the planning process to ensure best practices are met throughout the entire sweepstakes marketing process. Sponsors need to ensure sufficient lead times are in place allowing for the lawyers to confirm that every aspect of a sweepstakes, contest or giveaway, on any platform, is defensible. Just as it's important for an entrant to read the rules, it's just as important for a sponsor to ensure the rules are properly written.

ೞೞ

TIP: Be sure to frequently check http://bit.ly/QuebecRegie for updates to the Régie's Publicity Contest Notice online PDF as the regulations change without notice.

Brenda Pritchard and Susan Vogt of Gowling Lafleur Henderson (www.gowlings.com) are two of Canada's leading advertising and marketing lawyers. (Contesting law falls within this specialty.) Their book, *Advertising and Marketing Law in Canada*, is a must read for all advertising and marketing professionals. They give a good overview of who is responsible for the rules in Canada, especially Quebec and why most Canadian promotions are void in Quebec.

The Ground Rules:
Every contest and incentive program is a contract between the promoter and participants. The terms of the contract are set out in either the contest rules or the terms and conditions of the offer. Most advertisers would not sign a business contract without careful attention to the legal side, but many people in marketing do not realize the legal implications of the contracts they regularly extend to consumers in the form of contests and incentive programs.

Contest rules must be comprehensive, and clearly communicated to consumers. The same applies to the terms and conditions of other incentive programs. If these contracts are incomplete or poorly drafted, and you have to rely on them in court, be aware of the legal rule of *contra preferendum*. Any ambiguity in a contract is interpreted against the party who drafted the contract--in this case, the promoter or advertiser.

To assist in understanding the potential issues and in weeding through the legal boilerplate, we have included draft contest rules, set later in this chapter. In a good set of rules or terms and conditions, every word is there for a reason.

Equally important is the applicable legislation. Promotional contests are governed by the *Competition Act*, the *Criminal Code* and Quebec's *Act respecting lotteries, publicity contests and amusement machines*.

Before discussing the law, we will briefly define some terms. Contests can be divided into two broad categories: skill contests and contests where prizes are awarded randomly. Until recently, skill contest--where winners are selected by experienced judges based on the contestants' skill at story-writing, photography, *etc.*—were very common.

Contests where winners are chosen at random include: sweepstakes, where prizes are awarded by random draw; seeded games (including Coke's "under the bottle cap" promotions and Tim Hortons' "Roll Up the Rim to Win"), where prizes are randomly seeded on game cards or on-pack, and participants must scratch, unpeel or otherwise reveal the prize area to discover whether they have won a prize; online instant win games where consumers enter a code number (usually obtained on-pack); and "match and win" games where participants must collect game pieces to spell specific words or match the pieces of a puzzle. "Match and win" games are usually structured to include "rare pieces", which make the odds of winning a major prize astronomical. There are as many varieties of random contests as marketers can devise.

Quebec:
Whether or not to include Quebec residents in a contest is often determined by whether you want to deal with the Régie. The Régie has jurisdiction over all contests which are "launched to the public" in Quebec. Thus, "employee" contests are not governed by the Régie, but, generally, trade promotions are. In most cases, franchisees and their employees are covered by this exemption. All "public contests" which are open to Quebec residents must be registered with the Régie unless the total prize value is less than $2,000. You should note, however, that if the prize pool is less than $2,000 but more than $100, you will still have to pay the "duty" to the Régie.

Complete information on registering your contest with the Régie is available at <http://www.racj.gouv.qc.ca>. If you need to deal with the Régie, you should consider the following:

(a) Who should file the registration documents? If anyone other than the sponsor or the sponsor's lawyer registers the contest they will have to file a proxy.

(b) Contest rules and contest-related advertising must be filed with the Régie 10 days before the start date. Ideally, these should be filed in French unless the contest will be carried only in English media, but the Régie will accept English ads that have not been translated yet.

(c) The Régie assesses the duty at the rate of 3 per cent of total prize value for a national contest or 10 per cent of the value of prizes allocated to Quebec residents. If the contest is a scratch and win or otherwise seeded, you only have to pay duty on the value of the prizes you estimate will be redeemed. Depending on the value of the prizes, duty and the registration documents are due 10-30 days before the contest start date. The usual penalty for late filing is interest on the late payment of duty.

(d) If the value of any prize offered to Quebec residents exceeds $5,000, or the total prizes offered to Quebec residents exceeds $20,000, you will have to file a security bond.

(e) Within 60 days of the contest's draw date, you will have to file a detailed final report (*i.e.*, a winners' list) with the Régie.

(f) You cannot amend or withdraw a contest in Quebec without the Régie's approval.

(g) The Régie requires you to keep all contest entry forms for 120 days following the draw date.

(h) If a contest falls within the Régie's jurisdiction, the rules and advertising must include specific clauses that are not required in the rest of Canada. These are set out in sections 5 and 6 of the *Rules respecting publicity contests*.

(i) Recently, the Régie has required the name of the contest sponsor's contact, even if the sponsor's office is not located in Quebec.

(j) While previously "skill contests" were not considered "publicity contests" subject to the Régie's jurisdiction, that position has been reversed—so all contests conducted by a sponsor with prizes over $100 (total), whether all skill or partial skill and chance, must registered.

This material has been sourced, with permission, from Chapter 8 of Pritchard, Vogt: Advertising and Marketing Law in Canada, 4th Edition (LexisNexis Canada Inc.) (2012)

STORY: Why having a government regulatory body can be helpful when something goes wrong.

෨ඥ

Melanie—Repentigny, QC

Many companies run contests that conclude at the end of the year. It turns out I had entered a contest that ended December 28th. The following March I received a letter from the Régie asking if I had received my prize.

I had not.

It turns out I won a trip to Turkey! Before contacting the Régie back, I thought I would contact the sponsor first. I Googled my name and discovered the sponsor had announced my name as the winner in an association newsletter.

It took me several calls to track down my prize. I contacted the newsletter to find out how they got my name. They told me to contact the provincial association. They told me to contact the television show that sponsored the contest. I Googled the show and found the producer's contact information.

I called and he was surprised I didn't know I had won. I wish I had thought to ask him why they didn't call me. He was surprised I didn't watch the show live when they announced my name, but it was the holidays and I was busy with family gatherings.

He gave me the name of the travel agent who was ready to book my trip. When I called she was wondering why I had not called earlier.

The trip was fantastic and I have to thank the Régie for their diligence on large prizes. Otherwise I may never have known I won.

Unfortunately, the Régie no longer sends out those letters as they notified, not only me, but many of my friends, of several "missing" prizes.

෨ඥ

I DIDN'T READ THE RULES

As my then-husband loves car racing, so when we were married, whenever I would find a racing contest I would enter. In 2006 a local paper was hosting a contest giving away tickets to the Molson Grand Prix. I skimmed the rules entering us daily; myself via paper form found in the paper and Craig via the online form.

I will never forget the winning phone call. I was told I was the lucky winner of Silver Weekend Grandstand Passes, but to win the grand prize of a private lunch with Bret "The Hitman" Hart I had to participate in a sumo wrestling contest. I nearly turned down the prize, but I thought to myself, "You didn't read the rules, just like you tell everyone else to, so suck it up and go wrestle."

Right after I won Craig said to me, "I read in a book that you should always read the rules." I replied, "I know. I read the same book."

When I arrived at the wrestling ring I discovered two of the four winners didn't show up so I would only have to wrestle one person to win! The other competitor turned out to be Frank; a very fit man, who was a good 8" taller and good 50lbs heavier than me. Hmmm…this was going to be a challenge. I didn't know how big a challenge until I wriggled into the sumo suit. Frank fit into his suit just fine. Since I am only 5'3" and 140lbs the suit was swimming on me. Then came the helmet. It was so big that I couldn't see. So I put my baseball cap on to hold the helmet up. That didn't work, so they finally got a t-shirt, folded it up, put it on my head and squished the helmet on. I could finally see. We then had to stand, all suited up, in the hot sun for 10 minutes while we waited for Bret to arrive. It was going to be the best of three. Once the match started I realized, not only was Frank bigger than me, he had also sumo wrestled before. I was in trouble. In no time he had knocked me down and slammed me. Thank goodness the suits are all padding. I didn't feel a

thing. OK, so now I had to win or it was all over. In the second round I was able to maneuver around Frank a bit more and give him a few good pushes but not enough to knock him down. He gave me one really good push, I fell backwards and my helmet got stuck in between the ropes. When he slammed me the helmet

43

came loose and covered my face. At first everyone thought I got hurt but I was fine. (This is when I figured out why they have the competitors sign a long release waiver before stepping into the ring.) Frank had won lunch with Bret Hart. He was very happy. Frank and I had a chance to talk after the match. It turns out he was a fellow contestor. He inspired me to finally follow through on an idea I had for over a year; to start Canada's first official contesting club. (See chapter, Join a Sweepstakes Club, for clubs in your area.)

I am sad to report this picture of Frank accepting his prize is the only one I have of the sumo wrestling event as my camera batteries died. (Or maybe that was a good thing?) You can the original version of my adventure here: http://bit.ly/TWEv2i15

The joy of being part of the sweepstakes community is seeing friendly faces again and again. I had the pleasure of running into Frank at another winning event two years later: http://bit.ly/JackJohnJoe

I will repeat my #1 sweeping tip because it is so important:
Read The Official Rules *and* Follow Them!

"Luck is believing you're lucky."
Tennessee Williams

FIVE WAYS TO ENTER

There are five ways a company will allow entries into their giveaways:

- in-store/in-person;
- radio/phone-in;
- mail-in;
- online/Internet;
- cellphone (text messaging, Instagram and in-app).

You will notice as you read a giveaway's official rules that sometimes you can enter using more than one entry method or that they have been combined to give you one entry. An example of alternative entry methods would be entering either by mail or online. An example of combined entry methods would be to text-in an entry that gives you a code to enter online.

The secret to the hobby of sweepstaking is to make it your own. It is meant to be fun, not work. Try different entry methods, visit various websites, subscribe to a few newsletters, etc. Play with it. Find what you like, what makes you feel good (See chapter, Attracting Luck.), and what brings in wins for you. Everyone could use more dreams, fun and excitement in their lives.

NOTE: There are more resources available than I could possibly write about in this book. Included are the people, companies, websites, groups and forums that wished to participate in this book. The Internet is also a very "fluid" place and websites come and go in a heartbeat. Remember to check www.contestqueen.com under Resources for additional and frequently updated contesting or sweepstaking resources.

IN-STORE

In-store sweepstakes are generally: a fill-in entry form sweepstakes, a swipe your loyalty card giveaway, a game piece collection style promotion, a seeded sweepstakes or a TV/radio remote.

The entry form and loyalty card style of promotions are designed to draw in foot traffic and potential sales into the store, or near the product sponsoring the promotion, as well as to expand the store's mailing list. They are usually found at the front of the store or near the cash register. The odds in these types of promotions are usually good since many times the prize is one per store, the entry period is short, it has not been advertised to the general public, except maybe the stores newsletter subscribers, and the people that do enter, generally only fill out one entry form.

TIP: Do not help yourself to the entire entry pad, fill the entry forms out at home and then go back to the store to enter them. The sweepstakes may have unlimited entries, however, it is on the edge of cheating and it is not good karma. (See chapter, Attracting Luck.)

If the rules are available, it is important to read them. If a major retail chain is holding the entry form method of drawing, the rules are usually printed on the back of the entry form or posted near the entry box. If it is loyalty card swipe, game piece collection or seeded contests, the rules are usually found online or at the Customer Service counter. Major retailers have been known to limit entries to one entry per person or one entry per household for the entire chain. They also do not necessarily pool all the entry forms together. I have seen promotions where the entries are filled out country wide, and then a particular store is chosen; a name is then selected from the entry box in that specific store. Another method of selection is that a few entry forms from each store are sent to the company's head office, and the winner is selected from those entry forms only.

Game sweepstakes originally were only conducted with the in-store method of entry. With the advent of Internet sweepstakes, some game sweepstakes now involve purchasing or mailing away for PIN codes (Personal Identification Number) or game pieces to be entered on a specific online sweepstakes website.

NOTE: PIN code based sweepstakes are being run more frequently by sponsor companies because it makes it easy for the average consumer to enter once while at the same time making it harder for those that make a habit of entering multiple times.

> Game sweepstakes are the fastest growing form of sweepstakes today. The major reason for their popularity is that a sweepstakes player participates in finding out whether or not he or she has won a prize.

> Some sweepstakes players view game sweepstakes as the fast food version of "regular" sweepstakes—they remove some of the mystery from sweepstakes. In random draw sweepstakes, one fills out and submits an entry, not certain whether the entry will win or lose. Players are only notified later if they win. There is no way to

know whether you have lost a sweepstakes unless you request a winners list. (We've never heard of a judging organization that notifies the losers.)

In game sweepstakes, the number of prizes and the number of entries are predetermined. The number of entries is determined by the number of game pieces printed. (Only a fixed percentage of the total number of game pieces printed are winners.) The number of people playing a game sweepstakes has no effect on your chances of winning. Either you get a winning card or you do not.

Not all game sweepstakes are the same. There are five types of game sweepstakes: collect, match, decode and instant-win predetermined and instant-win probability.

Collect. To win the collect game sweepstakes, the entrant must collect game pieces (of which usually one or more are rare) to spell a word, build a picture, and so forth. Many potential players unwittingly discard the rare pieces.

Match. Match game sweepstakes usually involve matching a number or picture from a game piece to a list of winning selections. Typically, the winning selections are posted in retail stores, or can be obtained through the mail.

Decode. Decode game sweepstakes usually instruct the entrant to take his or her game piece to a special decoding display in a store to see if it is a winner. The game pieces are always scrambled so that it cannot be read without the "special" decoder. Some new-fangled decode sweepstakes require computer equipment to play. In 1989 K Mart put bar codes on store flyers which customers brought to K Mart stores to be scanned. The computer announced if and what the customer won.

Instant-Win Predetermined. Predetermined instant-win sweepstakes usually feature a game piece from which you scratch off a covering layer, that reveals any prize that may have been won. For example, in scratching a card three panels may be revealed; if all match, the card is a winner. How you scratch the game piece has no affect because the outcome is predetermined.

It is sometimes possible to differentiate winning and losing game pieces prior to playing if the pieces were printed separately. One can look for slight differences such as a filled in letter "e" or a stray dot that might appear only on winning game pieces.

Instant-Win Probability. In probability games, every piece is a potential winner if scratched or played properly. For example, Applian Way Pizza ran a probability instant-win game in which ten spots were covered with a film layer. Two of the ten spots carried matching prizes. If the player could uncover the matching spots with only two scratches, he or she would win the prize indicated. Every game card was a potential winner of $5 to $5,000.

Copyright ©1990 by Jeffrey & Robin Sklar. Extract from Winning Sweepstakes published by Sebell Publishing Company Inc.

I like to support the sweepstakes sponsor by buying their products to get the PIN codes, especially since the price of postage is now higher than the cost of purchasing many products. When companies deem their promotions are successful, they will keep running them and possibly, even run more. However, it is not healthy to eat too much chocolate, soda pop, sugary cereal, etc. My advice is to balance out the cost of postage vs. the cost of the product and the impact on your health to determine how much to buy. Occasionally I may even go PIN code hunting, but since iCoke (aka MyCokeRewards in the U.S.) was closed in Canada, it's a very infrequent occurrence.

In the book The Prize Winner of Defiance Ohio, Dortha Schaefer takes Evelyn Ryan to the city dump to get "qualies" (Qualifiers such as labels, box tops, UPCs, etc.) I am not that ambitious, but in the past I used to drive by many product containers with PIN codes on them in blue bins on recycle day and think to myself, "Look at all those winning opportunities just being thrown away!" Now don't let those potential wins go to waste. Weather permitting, and depending on which PIN code contests are running, on recycle day take a walk around your neighborhood with a plastic bag to collect the soda pop bottle lids and a pair of scissors to cut off any codes on bottles or boxes. Not only will you be getting exercise, but possibly collecting the trip of a lifetime, a big screen TV or a new car!

TIP: Get your family and friends to help you win. One of our sweepstakes club members finds a bag of "garbage" outside her door once a week. Her neighbor saves anything with a PIN code on it and gives it to her since they do not enter. In return she passes back little wins such as movie passes or CDs.

Always read the rules to see what the NPE is and you can then plot your winning strategy. Legally, the odds are the same if you bought the product or send away for a NPE.

Seeded sweepstakes are the hardest to win because it involves finding the winning piece in thousands or even millions of product containers (e.g. bottle cap liners, toilet rolls, talking cans, etc.). Charlie and the Chocolate Factory (by Ronald Dahl) is the most famous, and fictional, example of a seeded sweepstakes. The children had to be lucky enough to find a golden ticket in the chocolate bar packaging to win an invitation to the chocolate factory.

NOTE: There is a difference between collect-to-win and seeded sweepstakes even though both have very rare winning pieces, coupons, notifications, etc. In the collect-to-win you get a game piece(s) with every purchase and you hope you get one of the rare winning pieces. In seeded sweepstakes you do not collect anything. You just hope you are lucky enough to find the winning certificate, notification, etc.

Second Chance Drawings

In the United States sponsors often hold second chance drawings to award unclaimed prizes once their primary promotion has closed. Since it is not a legal requirement in Canada for all prizes to be awarded, second chance drawings are not as frequent.

Not every promotion will hold a second chance drawing, so it is important to read the rules to determine how the judging agency or sweepstakes management company will be handling any unclaimed prizes.

TIP: Many scratch lottery tickets have a second chance drawing attached to them. Check your state's lottery website for details. (See section, Lotteries.)

Second chance drawings are usually held in conjunction with instant win sweepstakes which include: instant win games in which you are told immediately if you won (either online or on a physical product), collect and win games (where you collect game pieces to complete a certain set) and match and win games (where you match a symbol or word to a posted list of winners).

Once the promotion is over, many sponsors still want to award those prizes which were not claimed during the regular promotional period. On average only about 30% of the prizes are awarded in an instant win promotion, with the exception being Tim Horton's Roll Up The Rim annual contest that has an over 90% claim rate.

Sponsor's count on the low claim rate because even if they are awarding the larger prizes in a second chance drawing, they do not have to award all the prizes. This allows them to either: offer larger prizes on a smaller promotional marketing budget or leave enough funds in their budget to run another instant win sweepstakes.

This is why, in most cases, these second chance entries are the easiest to win. There are usually large prize pools left over to be given away. The prizes go unclaimed for the following reasons:

- they are still sitting on the store shelf after the promotional period has ended;
- the product has been purchased, but is sitting in the pantry of someone's home;
- the product was purchased, but the game pieces were tossed in the trash by a non-sweeper;
- the game piece was checked, but misplaced or tossed out in error.

TIP: Look around when eating at a fast food restaurant, a ballgame or the movies. How many cups, bottles, bags or boxes are left around with the games pieces still intact? They will end up in the trash if not collected by someone, so go claim those winning opportunities for yourself!

When you see a sweepstakes offering a second chance drawing, immediately check to see how many prizes will be available at the end of the promotion if any are left unclaimed. In some cases, they only draw names for the unclaimed Grand Prize or largest prizes, such as when the lower level prizes are some of their own products or when they feel they can reuse the products in another promotion at a later date. Only send in one or two entries to the second chance drawing if there are only one or two possible winners in this part of the promotion. If there are a lot of prizes being given away, then send in more entries based either on the amount of possible prizes to be won or your comfort level. My preference is to send in 10-20 entries, depending on the prize, but I know others who will send in hundreds.

NOTE: Just because there are hundreds of prizes being awarded in the main promotion, it doesn't mean there will be hundreds available for the second chance drawing. Again, be sure to read the rules under the Unclaimed Prizes or Second Chance headings in the sponsor's rules. Then make your decision on how many entries to send in.

Sometimes you don't need to do anything to enter a second chance drawing. Those entering promotions online and playing interactive games may discover when they lose on the initial step of the promotion that they are automatically entered into a second chance drawing.

TIP: While grocery shopping check the aisles for products that have game pieces or codes inside the packaging. Read the rules and see what the main and second chance drawing options are. In many cases, after the main promotion has ended, you will still see sweepstakes labeled products for sale on the shelf. Depending on the main and second chance drawing dates, your odds of winning in the second chance drawing may be very good. Either that or the product on the shelf is so old, you may wish to skip purchasing it altogether.

I always encourage those new to the hobby to enter the sweepstakes and second chance drawings with lots of prizes being given away. The prizes may not necessarily be big ticket items, but it is a great way to begin to win.

STORY: You are never too young to start entering sweepstakes, raffles or contests.

≈∞≈

Al—Dearborn, MI

My first entry into entering contests came when I was 12 years old. I lived in Hingham, MA and my father decided to take the whole family on a trip to Portland, ME to see my mother's sister. On the way (we went by train) we stopped over at Old Orchid Beach, ME. They had an amusement park and a beach. We were to stay there for the day and catch the late train to Portland. My mother saw this brand new steam iron (it had just come on the market) and since she did laundry for a living, really wanted it. My father wasn't much of a gambler, so I borrowed $1 from him and bought a chance to win the steam iron. I won the iron and I also won a candy guessing game. That was the start of my interest in entering contests. It wasn't until about 1960 before I began entering contests fairly regularly and I have been sweeping ever since. I'm still looking for a car and I know it is coming.

≈∞≈

RADIO/PHONE-IN

Radio contests are designed to keep a listener hooked for their next opportunity to call-in and win. When larger prizes are given away, they are designed to keep listeners hooked for days or weeks at a time. You will generally find the larger the market, the better the prizes. This is because in larger cities, they have more listeners; therefore they can charge their advertisers more and have more funds available for bigger promotions. It is usually also more difficult to "get through" on the contest phone line as more people are trying to qualify or win the giveaway.

NOTE: You can listen to many radio stations from around the globe online. Be aware: 1) there is usually minor time delay, a few seconds, between what is aired live on the radio and what is aired over the Internet and radio apps, and 2) many radio stations require you to pick-up your prize in person at the station. If you live in Toronto, you may enjoy the music from the Chicago radio station but you may be wasting your time trying to win their promotions.

In the past when a radio station gave away a prize you had to be the 7th, 10th, 25th, etc. caller through on the contest phone line to win the prize. As the Internet became more popular, radio stations began to add online sweepstakes as a way to "level the playing field" because if you were terrible at dialing-in, everyone could fill out an online entry form.

More and more radio stations are implementing online loyalty listener clubs in addition to their standard phone-in radio contests and online entry sweepstakes.

There are two types of clubs: 1) be an online member to be able to enter, or 2) membership requires you to accumulate points by listening for codes then return to the station's website, enter the code and rack up points. Many also have other methods of accumulating points such as online games and trivia for additional club points. With your accumulated points you could bid for prizes or enter into sweepstakes.

Be aware that before you become a member of your favorite radio station's loyalty listener club not all stations' sweepstakes are open to the listeners of only one radio station. Since there are very few independently owned radio stations, the conglomerates are combining their marketing budgets and online efforts. You are now no longer entering sweepstakes competing against those within the immediate listening area, but within all the markets in which the parent company owns radio stations.

TIP: Follow a radio station's social media account as they share code words, text-in times, cues to call in, etc. which increase your odds of winning.

The first sweepstakes I can remember entering was a radio contest to see Burton Cummings at Hamilton Place. I stood in the kitchen for ages dialing on a rotary dial phone hoping to be the fourth caller through. I was so excited when I won those tickets. I was only fourteen so my mom had to go down and pick up the tickets. She also went with me to the concert. We sat fourth row center. I felt so grown-up and so lucky!

With life getting busier and busier, I find I am rarely entering radio call-in contests. I always seem to be driving or on a call when the announcer plays the cue to call-in. At the same time, I know there are many people who have tremendous luck calling-in-to-win.

STORY: Bea had a really good tip on how she "gets through" on her local radio station's contest line. She won a trip to see U2 in Los Angeles. Try this method of entering and decide for yourself if it is for you.

৪১০৫৪

Bea—Toronto, ON

The redial button on the phone that I qualified on is really fast. I have a cordless phone and another phone that is more expensive but slow in redialing. The main suggestion I have is before you hear the cue to call is to start calling. With this contest I had to call after hearing two U2 songs. In between they placed the cue but I literally started a couple seconds before. Never give up. I know that radio call-in contests can be more difficult but be persistent. I was going to give up since I didn't qualify the first weekend. I could hardly believe it when the DJs called me Monday morning to tell me I had won. I had forgotten to set my alarm and literally woke up seconds before the phone rang. We had an awesome time at the concert.

৪১০৫৪

TIP: Activate the auto-redial feature on your cellphone when calling in to radio stations.

I did have great luck with one call-in-to-win contest. When my daughter was an infant I was able to call-in to qualify my then-husband for a 'Guy's Get-Away'. It was 7:00am on a Sunday morning. I was breast-feeding my daughter in front of the computer while I entered sweepstakes online. In the background I had the radio on listening for my cue to call-in. When I heard the signal, I dialed right away. I was caller one. I thought, "Damn, I dialed too fast." Then I thought, "I should try again." I was caller two. I looked at the phone puzzled. I called back. I was caller three, four, five and six! I don't think anyone else was listening at that hour. I knew then we were going to win. Since it was a male oriented prize I gave the announcer Craig's name.

The next morning was the big draw. I was up at 5:00am feeding my daughter and heard which DJ was announcing that morning. Then I went back to bed turning the ringer on our phone back on. (It had been turned off since our daughter had been born.) At 7:10am the phone rang. I picked it up and sure enough it was the DJ. I screamed "WE WON! WE WON!" shaking poor Craig awake as he was sound asleep. He sat up bewildered and I handed him the phone. Once they confirmed it was Craig and told him he was going to Florida to be a judge in the Miss Hawaiian Tropics Bikini Contest State Finals. We had a ball. I don't think we could have fit any more fun into three

53

days. All his friends wanted to know where they could find a wife like me (or like the bikini models!).

TIP: To increase your odds of dialing in and getting through, try listening to less popular radio stations.

STORY: Radio stations run fantastic promotions that involve their listeners allowing them to possibly participate in an adventure.

ℬⳐ

Joe—Warren MI

Two DJs from our local radio station hold an annual Adult Easter Egg Hunt. I usually cannot attend because they hold it on the morning of Good Friday and I work. In 1998, I had the opportunity because I was off work. That year they had one egg containing $1000. When I showed up they had 1000 Easter Eggs scattered on a football field and were putting those of us who were going after them around the outside of the field.

They started to announce the rules, stating that there were over 2000 people surrounding the field and only 1000 eggs so there would be some people who would not receive an egg. They said that in five minutes they would fire a cannon, and at that sound we could go after the eggs.

I told my friends, Diana, Mike, and Patti to look around at all the people. They looked like they were so much faster than I was so I had to have a plan if I wanted to get any eggs.

With less than five minutes, I came up with the following plan: I predicted that everyone is going to stop and pick up the first egg they came to so I wouldn't even think about that close egg, I was concentrating on the eggs in the center of the field. Sounds good right?

After what seemed like an eternity, the cannon finally fired and we were off. What I didn't plan on was a couple to my right running while holding hands. They ran into my path and the woman fell pulling the man down with her, right in front of me. With my catlike reactions, I did an OJ Simpson style leap over them. Well, either I didn't quite clear them, or they were already standing up, but I tripped up on his back.

I ended up doing a belly flop onto the ground and scooping eggs in as I slid across the grass. While over a thousand people did not get any eggs, I got five. I didn't get the $1000 egg. Two of my eggs contained candy, one egg had a $20 gift certificate to a grocery store, one egg had a $25 gift certificate to a restaurant and the last egg had $50 cash in it. Not bad for a guy who doesn't have to stuff his Santa suit.

෨෦෬

There are two adages given to the hobby of sweepstaking: the 3Ps and 4Cs. Every sweeper needs **P**atience, **P**ersistence, and **P**ostage and every sweeper wants to win **C**ash, **C**ars, **C**omputers and **C**ruises.

MAIL-IN

The topic of mail-in (aka snail mail) sweepstakes is vast. This section could be a book unto itself. I do not plan to rewrite what many others have already written on the topic. I will briefly skim the topic to give you an overview.

There are virtually no mail-in contests left in Canada. I have not seen an Official Entry Blank (OEB) in stores since 2006. The only mail-ins are the ones attached to a purchase-to-enter giveaway and in accordance with promotional law the sponsors must include a No Purchase Entry option (NPE). A NPE mail-in will require you to send in anything from; simply your name and email, to your full contact information, loyalty card number and a 50, 100, 250 or 500 word essay on why you love or need their products or service.

TIP: If a sweepstakes asks for an essay with a specific word count (e.g. 250-word essay) type it out on your computer first, using a program like Microsoft Word, and using the WORD COUNT feature to get the precise word count. Then depending on the rules, you can either print it out and submit it or copy out by hand what you have just typed.

Can I Force a Purchase?
In Canada, unless it is a skill contest, you clearly cannot force a purchase to enter a contest if the prize consists of "goods, wares or merchandise". If the prize is a service or cash, and the cost to enter is *more* than the prize, you *can* force a purchase. If, for example, a person had to buy a car to enter to win the cash equivalent of the car purchase less $100, the contest would be legal. However, this only works because the person is not winning a *whole* car, which is clearly merchandise. If you can't fit into these limited exceptions, it is best to add a no-purchase requirement (as in the U.S.) given equal integrity to the no-purchase entrant.

This material has been sourced, with permission, from Chapter 22 of Pritchard, Vogt: Advertising and Marketing Law in Canada, 4[th]Edition (LexisNexis Canada Inc.) (2012)

As the sweepstakes laws are different in the United States than in Canada, mail-in giveaways are still available although, they are more difficult to find as companies prefer online based promotions. This is a straight bottom line decision: it is far less expensive to run an online promotion than a mail-in promotion. The upside for sweepers is that there are fewer people entering mail-in giveaways, so the odds are getting better for those who do. The easiest way to find mail-in sweepstakes is to subscribe to a newsletter that has mail-in sweepstakes as part of its offering. (See section, Newsletters.)

There is a debate within the contest community regarding the best way to win when a giveaway has both an online and mail-in option. My stance has always been if a sweepstakes has both always use the Internet option, because many companies treat mail-in entries like Internet entries by either coding them or opening the envelope and typing the information into the computer system. You are wasting time and money mailing in to these types of promotions. It is only beneficial if the rules state one online entry and unlimited mail-in entries. The other option is to do both, following the official rules of course, to maximize your odds as you do not know if the winner will be selected via the mail-in entries or the online ones. Try both and see what works best for you.

Remember, it's always important to read the rules so you know how many members of the household can enter, how often you can enter, the contest end date and how they would like the entry form sent in.

My personal favorites are one entry per person or one entry per household sweepstakes because: 1) everyone has an equal chance to win and 2) they take far less time to enter.

RECOMMENDED READING: Author Steve Ledoux dedicates a chapter in his book How to Win Lotteries, Sweepstakes and contests in the 21st Century dedicated to mail-in sweepstakes.

Postal Standards

Both the United States Postal Service (USPS) and Canada Post (CP) have set-out envelope and postcard addressing standards (along with other standards) that should be followed to ensure your mail-in entries are delivered properly. This is especially important if you choose to decorate, embellish or create your own envelopes. Size, weight and other factors may affect the amount of postage required or the mailability of your item.

For addressing format, location guidelines and other requirements. You should visit the USPS website at: http://bit.ly/USPSStandards and CP at:

http://bit.ly/CPStandards. Check back periodically as postal standards can and do change.

Some people like to decorate or embellish their entry envelopes feeling it will increase their odds of winning. Again, ensure you adhere to USPS and CP standards and do not draw, color, paint, glue or place stickers within the areas that are to remain clear. This will help ensure your entry is delivered properly. Also, keep all embellishments flat and do not use raised or puffy stickers, glue, paint etc. as they could catch in the postal machines, ruining your entry. This includes making sure that all of the edges of the envelope are smooth and straight. The last thing you want is to spend hours on a special envelope, only to have it be accidentally ripped open by a letter sorting machine.

TIP: Use a standard #10 business-sized envelope for your mail-in entries. Many companies I interviewed said if the envelope is too large, it will not fit into the drawing drum. The entry would then either be removed and placed into a smaller envelope or discarded altogether.

Postcards

Many sweepstakes ask you to send in your entry on a postcard.

A standard postcard is 4¼ x 6. If a sweepstakes asks for a 3 x 5 postcard, you can cut a regular unstamped postcard down and place it in an envelope. A 3 x 5 postcard is too small to mail according USPS mailing guidelines. The minimum is 3½ x 5. Often companies request a 3 x 5 postcard in error or misuse the term "postcard" when they mean an index card.

As long as the rules do not specifically state the required postcard's dimensions, another option is to use shaped postcards, although additional postage may apply. These are usually sold alongside regular postcards. They are a bit more expensive: however the card's surface area is generally much larger than a standard postcard and the varied sides could provide a better opportunity to be selected.

TIP: Turn the postcard vertically and write the FROM information perpendicular to the TO information. I used to do this because a friend of mine was a postal employee and told me the machines send the card to whichever address they "read" first. If the FROM address is sideways it will not be read.

RESOURCES GUIDE
A = American
C = Canadian
U = United Kingdom
I = International

Sweeping Supplies

Even though mail-in sweepstakes are quickly disappearing, there are still some suppliers providing contestors with a wide variety of unique and fun sweeping supplies.

NOTE: I have only featured a few suppliers here. Additional resources can be found under Resources at www.contestqueen.com

CJ's Designs   A

cjenvelopes@yahoo.com

Carolyn Sayward started her business in 1999 after she suffered a stroke. She originally designed the envelopes for her husband, Al, to use for his sweepstakes. Al gave a few samples to his fellow club members and their business was born. Even though Carolyn passed away in 2009, Al chose to keep their business open.

CJ's specializes in computer generated graphic designs. They have every theme you can think of, including: Animals, Sports, People, Holidays, Trips and Automotive. Mail or email Al to request an order form.

CJ's Designer Envelopes
P.O. Box 463131
Mt. Clemens, MI 48046-3131

K.C. Supplies   A

www.kcsupplies.net

Karen Weix has been a sweeper for over 20 years. She started with a friend at a Rebate Club. A fellow member kept talking about all the trips she was winning and invited Karen and her friend to attend the next meeting. It was a year before they attended and couldn't figure out why they waited so long to start sweeping! Many years later she has won everything from fully paid vacations, to going to the Olympics, tickets to sport games, plays and concerts, as well as winning cash and cars!

Karen started K.C. Supplies at an Annual National Sweepstakes Convention. She reserved a vendor table alongside a friend and they began with a few supplies and some small raffles. Each year, as the convention grew so did K.C. Supplies. Customers now have access to a variety of envelopes, postcards, papers, stickers and other must-have sweeping supplies all year round by mail or online. Her sweeping supplies have helped bring luck and big wins to many of her customers, friends and sweeping buddies across the country.

She has been a member of the Illini Dream Team since she started sweepstaking, and currently is one of the board members.

K. C. Supplies
368 Forest Preserve Drive
Wood Dale, IL 60191

Print My 3x5s   A

www.printmy3x5s.com

Jennifer Day began her hand printing service and her sweepstaking hobby almost at the same time in 1997. She hand prints your information on 3 x 5 cards and paper along with 4 x 6 postcards. Her prices include the cost of the paper, cards and postcards along with shipping. She also has digital themed #10 envelopes.

Jenn has always had very clear and neat handwriting. Her service is invaluable to those with poor handwriting or who have problems with their hands, as many sweepstakes request hand printed information. She gives away 100 hand printed papers every month. Check her website for details.

Jennifer Day
3184 Lindenwood Drive
Dearborn, MI 48120

TIP: You can use the travel and picture postcards on your sweepstaking goal chart or vision board. (See chapter; Attracting Luck.)

When we were married, in 2002, Craig and I had a GREAT win via mail. It was a promotion being held by a very popular fabric softener company. They had sent a sample to our house to try a new scent. Along with the sample was a mail-in entry to win a washer and dryer or a few other prizes. It was a one entry per household sweepstakes.

One day our mail carrier came to the door with a registered letter. I had won first prize: a $2,000 Roots (www.roots.com) gift certificate! I needed a new winter coat, and had never owned a leather jacket *and* a girl can never have too many purses!

It was mid-December when we won. I knew if I mailed the affidavit and release forms back in the enclosed envelope they could get lost or delayed in the Christmas mail. I chose to spend the money and couriered the forms back. That was a wise decision for two reasons: 1) I knew that it got there, and 2) they were able to send my gift certificates back to me right away. My Craig and I were able to buy far more than we normally would have because of the great Boxing Day sales.

NOTE: Boxing Day in Canada is December 26th and is our biggest retail sales day of the year, similar to Black Friday in the United States.

What I found ironic was that on the entry form they had asked my opinion on the new scent and I told them the truth. I did not like it, I thought it smelled like bubble gum and I would not buy this particular scent, ever! I still won and I do buy their original scent.

Newsletters

Newsletters were the first type of sweepstakes aggregate available to contest hobbyists. Back in the day they would be mailed out bi-weekly or monthly. Now they are also sent out via email and/or have an online component overlapping their services with the online aggregates (see section, Aggregates).

TIP: Follow all the resources on their social media accounts as the newsletters and aggregates post giveaways on their Timelines/feeds.

NOTE: All the newsletters listed are paid subscription publications. Please check with each publication for current subscription rates.

Best Publications   A

www.bestsweepstakes.com

Nick Taylor has been a sweeper for more than 30 years. He is very entrepreneurial and was looking for a new business idea. Like myself, Nick combined his love of the hobby and his business savvy and created Best Publications 20 years ago. Best Publications prints three newsletters: Best Sweepstakes Newsletter, Best Extra and Best Weekly. He launched a companion website over 10 years ago. Subscribers have access to new online sweepstakes links, a chat room, forum and regional sweepstakes.

Best Publications
PO Box 421163
Plymouth, MN 55442

Canadian Contests C

http://canadiancontests.com/

Canadian Contests Newsletter was founded in 1990 and offers a monthly mailed newsletter to subscribers. An emailed version is also available.

Lori Novak is the editor of Canadian Contests Newsletter and offers the reader information about: current contests, prizes and their value, how to enter, tips and tricks, along with any other information you need to win!

In addition to the newsletter the website offers: sample contests, winner's experiences and subscriber form. For a free sample of the latest issue, (one free newsletter sample per household) please contact Lori via email or mail.

Canadian Contests Newsletter
PO Box 23066
RPO McGillivray
Winnipeg, MB R3T 5S3

iWINContests   A

www.iwincontests.com

Tom Cavalli started sweeping in 2008 and started iWINContests in 2012 as another outlet for him to connect fellow sweepers along with being able to share the fun and excitement of the hobby.

iWINContests focuses specifically on best odds sweepstakes including: local, regional, limited entry or a high volume of prizes. It is a weekly newsletter with full details about each giveaway, clickable links and the occasional image. Tom specifically designed his publication to work in conjunction with other sweepstakes sources that list the more popular promotions and dovetails as well as an add-on to use with your current sourcing methods.

In 2016 the iWINContests website was revamped and Tom added: a text-to-win section, a skill-based contest page and a texting group you can join along with the ability to review past issues.

If you put 'Contest Queen' in the referred by section of the order form, you will get one month free!

TIP: Subscribe, or use, more than one sweepstakes sourcing method. Choosing different resources that focus on different areas of the hobby allow you to increase your odds of winning across a wide variety of platforms.

PowerSweepstaking   A

www.powersweepstaking.com

Ron Miller created PowerSweepstaking in 2007 as a way for fellow sweepers to enter sweepstakes faster and more efficiently. He felt scanning various online sites, groups and forums for promotions was too time consuming. Like myself, Ron has an extensive marketing background and he leveraged his knowledge to create a unique power entry system.

It was originally designed as an aggregate site. However, as technology moved forward the program couldn't keep up. By 2013 it would only work on Explorer and Firefox on a PC. In 2014 Ron ported his entire system over to an e-newsletter format. Now anyone on a PC or Mac, using any browser, can become a "power sweeper".

Like in the past, each member receives a daily email from Ron with all the sweepstakes they are to enter. There is no requirement to keep track of daily, weekly or monthly entries as PowerSweepstaking does it all for you.

Every member is also given the opportunity to send Ron up to five contest referral links. He promotes them in his newsletter and across all his social media outlets garnering the member additional entries.

Sweep-Easy   A

www.sweep-easy.com

After watching High Stakes Sweepers on TLC in 2011, Kate Thompson began entering sweepstakes and she was hooked after winning a signed Derek Jeter memorabilia.

Similar to myself, Kate combined her corporate skill set as a human resources manager with her hobby and came up with an organizational entry system to keep her on a winning track. After her sweepstakes club asked Kate to share her system, she thought that others would like it too and Sweep-Easy was born.

Unlike other newsletters Sweep-Easy arrives in your email inbox as a Microsoft Excel spreadsheet in both an .xls and .xlsx formats. The sweepstakes are broken up by entry type such as: Daily, Weekly, One Time Only, etc. Each sweepstakes has all the important applicable entry information including a clickable link.

SweepSheet® A

www.sweepsheet.com

SweepSheet® was launched in 1989 at the 1st Annual National Sweepstakes Convention. The current editor/owner of SweepSheet® is Patti Osterheld.

The SweepSheet® product includes a members-only paid website at www.sweepsheet.com and a bi-weekly newsletter available either by mail or as an online downloadable PDF.

Sections of the website include online sweepstakes, mail-in sweeps, text sweeps, restricted sweeps, social network sweeps, contests and Hot Flashes which are quick closing sweepstakes.

The bi-weekly newsletter sections include: Profile of a Fanatical Sweepstaker, Sweepstakes, Contests, In-Stores, Text Sweeps and Winners.

SweepSheet®
2413 W Algonquin Rd
Suite 429
Algonquin, IL 60102

Sweeping America A

www.sweepingamerica.com

Donna Ralph started Sweeping America in 2003 after her mom, Judy McCurdy an avid sweeper, suggested there had to be a way to get new Sweepstakes into people's hand more quickly.

Sweeping America specializes in mail-in sweepstakes (that are thriving), text entries, and a feature they call Gold Rush highlighting local, regional and restricted giveaways. Remember to keep your eye on your email inbox as Donna will send out an ALERT if entering a sweepstakes before the next Weekly Issue gives subscribers a greater opportunity to win.

Like a restaurant that is the best kept secret in your town, it's been quietly dishing up fabulous sweepstakes with better odds to hundreds of winning subscribers for over a decade.

Sweeping America
P.O. Box 211
Broken Arrow, OK 74013

This N' That Sweepstakes Club Newsletter   A

http://home.comcast.net/~tnte-mail/

In 2007 Carol McLaughlin, originally the owner of ANN-tics by Carol Sweepstakes Supplies took over publication of This N' That Newsletter. Unlike other publications that list sweepstakes, TNT, as it's affectionately known, is a collection of stories, tips, monthly drawings and email, pen pal, birthday clubs. It is a fun newsletter for those who do not have a sweepstakes club near them and would like to be part of the sweeping community. Even if you belong to a club it's a great way to enhance your hobby friendships. It's also the only "club" with members from all across the United States.

For a sample copy ($4) or if you want further information, visit her website.

Trader's Forum & Win A Contest   C

www.winacontest.com

Sylvia Gold started Trader's Forum in 1996. It is a cornucopia of anything manufacturers have to offer; coupons, rebates, bonus offers, contests, etc. and is mailed out once a month. Sample copies are available for $5.

Norman Holt started Win A Contest in 1997. It is sent out via email and regular mail. Sylvia was one of the first subscribers. In 2003 Norman became too ill to continue managing the newsletter, and Sylvia offered to take over. Unlike Traders Forum, it focuses only on contests. A mailed subscription is sent out every two weeks and the emailed version is sent out each week.

Win a Contest Newsletter
P.O. Box 21022
RPO Meadowvale
Mississauga, ON L5N 6A2

ONLINE

My favorite way to enter sweepstakes is via the Internet. It's fast, free, and there are more and more promotions online every day. The downside is, since it is so quick and easy to enter, more and more people have picked up Internet sweeping as a hobby. This means more competition, which affects the odds of winning.

The main focus of this book is on the fast growing method of Internet sweeping. In the following chapters, I will discuss the many ways you can use the Internet to enhance your hobby, including websites that feature portals to newsletters, forums where you can meet like-minded people online, sites that host online promotions, and methods of protecting yourself from identity theft, hackers and con artists plus how to protect your computer against viruses and spam.

NOTE: Do not fear monitored websites, forums or chat rooms. The monitoring is not designed to be "Big Brother," rather it is to prevent any type of online abuse and keeps the site safe and clean for its participants.

"You can't lose helping others win."
Anonymous

Aggregates

There are many websites, groups and blogs that either post contests and sweepstakes online directly or offer a link to a newsletter subscription. These are also known as sweepstakes or contest aggregates as they list and/or post legitimate contests, sweepstakes and giveaways.

The Balance: Contests A

www.thebalance.com/contests-4074034

Sandra Grauschopf has been running the Contests and Sweepstakes section of About.com since 2007. Entering sweepstakes is Sandra's passion, and she has been studying the hobby for more than a decade. In 2016 About.com Contests and Sweepstakes became a part of the Money Hacks section of The Balance, a daughter company of About.com that focuses on making personal finance accessible to everyone.

Sandra loves being able to share her knowledge and help others win, as well as the camaraderie the sweepstaking community offers. There are quite a few sweepstakes resources available on The Balance's Contests section including How-To articles (my favorite feature of the site) and listings of free sweepstakes and contests to enter. Sign-up for her free e-newsletter to receive sweepstakes news and updates twice every week.

Concoursweb C

www.concoursweb.com
NOTE: This site is in French.

Sacha Sylvain began entering contests because a close friend of his and her mother were contestors and winning on a regular basis. Being an avid "techie" and contestor, he created the Concoursweb site in 2002 because contests were not easy to find on the Internet and even more so in Quebec.

65

The site is updated daily with new contests and promotions. You can also sign-up for his free e-newsletter.

Contest Canada   C

www.contestcanada.com

Joe Head and David Larade launched Contest Canada in 2000. The contests posted on this site are only open to Canadians and has evolved to include all social networking giveaways. Some contests are province or city specific. A Canada/U.S. section has been added for contest open to both countries. Contests are vetted before posting so only giveaways whose prize value is over $100, or multiple opportunities to win, are listed on the site.

This is a paid contest site, with a 30-day free trial membership. Once you join, the site offers members a great bookmarking feature and Time Stamp allowing you to track contests (in a similar manner to my Internet contesting system). The website also includes a community forum.

ContestCanada.com
18 Millwood Drive
Lower Sackville, NS B4E 2V3

Contest Canada   C

www.contestcanada.net

Dan and Mike Skeen created Contest Canada in 2006 because they couldn't find a Canadian-focused site that categorized contests in a way they felt was easy to search. Contest Canada is updated daily with several new contests, and these are conveniently categorized in a way that makes them easy to find. Also, they were too old to play with Lego, so they decided to build websites instead.

Membership is 100% free, including GST. Membership allows one to post comments, join forum discussions, and sign up for their freshly-squeezed email updates.

They have a free daily email newsletter and RSS subscriptions that includes short summaries of all the contests posted for that day.

Visitors are welcome to post comments about any of the contests listed. Often these comments help other visitors understand and answer the entry requirements for the contest. They also have a discussion forum so visitors can start or join an online discussion on any topic that interests them.

Something that visitors love about the site is their tongue-in-cheek humour. Hey, you can't win contests every day, but if you can get a good laugh (or maybe a quick snicker) in the process then it's worthwhile.

Contest Chest A, C, U, I

www.contestchest.com

Evert Hoff originally owned a digital marketing company creating competitions for clients as part of their permission marketing plan. When he saw how well the promotions worked for his clients, in 2011 he decided to create the first global sweepstakes aggregate.

Membership is free and when you set-up your account you also set-up the contest filters. It will ensure you only see the competitions you are eligible for. Not only can you filter by country, province or state, but by promotion type and a variety of other contest fields.

Contest Chest encourages community participation by holding a monthly drawing for members that add new competitions to the site.

Be sure to follow Contest Chest on Facebook as there is a fan page for every country along with provinces and states.

TIP: Ensure whenever you sign up for emails coming from a major website you set your spam filters to accept emails from that organization. e.g. thewinningedge@contestqueen.com

Contest Girl A, C, U

www.contestgirl.com

Contest Girl is owned and operated by Linda Horricks. She started her website in 2006 and it lists sweepstakes and contests for the U.S., Canada and even some internationally. She stumbled across online sweepstaking after her sister won a cruise. When Linda began having success, her friends and family began to ask her for help. After emailing interesting sweepstakes to all these different people many times over, she saw a need for a better way of telling people about sweepstakes and for screening them to avoid the ones that were "scammy" or "spammy". Her husband, Martin, manages the technical aspects of the site, while Linda creates the content.

It is organized by location and entry frequency. There is even a feature called; My Contests, which allows you to select and organize the sweepstakes you are most interested in, saving you valuable entry time. There is also a Free Stuff section for those who like freebies.

Hypersweep   A

www.hypersweep.com

Scott Bourgeois started Hypersweep in 1999 at a time when there were relatively few sweepstakes focused websites. All visitors can browse their real-time database of online sweepstakes at no cost. Registered members have access to more robust features such as the ability to add sweepstakes to the site, earn entries into members-only drawings, and even earn free membership. The site automatically keeps track of your entries, and remembers the last time each sweepstakes was entered. Other advanced features include a personalized favorites list, a built-in form fill assistant, and even an automated entry system. Members can also interact through an instant message system. To help members avoid scams, all promotions are archived so you can confirm a winning notification is legitimate. Anyone can read the forum, but you must be a member to post messages. Members can also join a private mailing list with direct links to all new sweepstakes posted on the site the previous day.

Non-members who have purchased this book can also sign-up for the Hypersweep private mailing list by using the URL: www.hypersweep.com/CQ and the password CQFREE.

Online-Sweepstakes.com   A

www.online-sweepstakes.com

Online-Sweepstakes.com (OLS) was launched by Brent Riley in December of 1997. With a lifelong interest in computers and programming and a desire to learn how to design and program web sites, Brent decided to create a web site specializing in the listing of sweepstakes and contests for sweepers. An occasional sweeper himself, Brent set out with the goal of designing a sweepstakes site that could help improve sweepers' chances of winning as much as possible.

Over the last 10 years, OLS has become the largest sweepstakes directory and community of sweepers on the Internet. Featuring a fast, simple and easy to use website, a number of advanced and unique features that make finding, entering and winning sweepstakes easier and less time-consuming, and a very active message board of experienced and helpful sweepers, OLS is a community-centric sweepstakes site that helps its members and visitors win millions of dollars in cash and prizes every year.

OLS offers sweepers two levels of membership, Free and Premium. The Free membership gives you access to thousands of sweepstakes and most of the various features of the website. The Premium membership costs $30 per year and gives you access to a few thousand additional sweepstakes that are generally more difficult to find and less popular than those available with Free membership. Premium membership also includes an ad-free website, a few more advanced features that help you organize and track your entries and a unique tool called Shazam! that really helps speed up your online entries.

Quebec Concours   C

www.quebecconcours.com
NOTE: This site is in French.

Marc Gagnon started searching the Internet one night for contests open to Quebec residents because his girlfriend was frustrated at the lack of resources for Quebecois contesters. Along with Yassine Bichri (co-owner of www.sekooya.com) they launched Quebec Concours. The website has an extensive list of online contests, sweepstakes, lotteries and even surveys that pay participants. Although the site audience is mainly from Quebec, all Canadian provinces are welcome to participate in all of the listed contests since they are valid nationwide. Participants can win cash, vacations, cars, electronics, movies, gift certificates and more.

Sweepstakes.ca   A, C

www.sweepstakes.ca

Jeff Goodfield launched Sweepstakes.ca in 2006. He's an avid contestor and was frustrated trying to find sweepstakes and contests open to Canadians. After spending far too many hours reading the rules only to find out he was not eligible, Jeff decided to do something about it.

Sweepstakes.ca is not your average aggregate. It is very selective in the contests it lists making finding and entering giveaways easy.

Jeff also loves to share deals. The site features many value added offers, like -- free lottery tickets, daily deals, cheap auto loans, products for less than a buck a day -- along with links to its seven sister sites:

- WinGasoline.ca
- CanadaAutoFinance.ca
- CashSurveys.ca
- GiftRewards.ca
- ShopAndCompare.ca
- RiskFreeTrials.ca
- DealsAndDiscounts.ca

In a nutshell, Sweepstakes.ca not only offers you an easy way to find exclusive sweepstakes but a way to find freebies, daily deals, beauty product trials, samples, coupons, gift rewards, and other offers.

Sweepstakes Advantage & Sweepstakes Plus   A

www.sweepsadvantage.com
www.sweepstakesplus.com

Ken and Diane Carlos started in 1997 as a way to make ends meet. At that time, Diane was a stay-at-home mom looking for a way to supplement the family income. Entering sweepstakes looked like a good way to spend time while seeking employment. When the wins actually started showing up, they got the idea to start a sweepstakes website of their own. It felt good to create and offer something they believed in and offer to people at no cost. It was the perfect fit and has become one of their greatest achievements in life.

Membership to Sweepstakes Advantage is free. Members are eligible to enter exclusive SA Members Only Sweepstakes. There are also many useful online tools for members such as: Sweepscheck, My Sweepstakes, SweepsPop and Sweepstakes Notes. On average 150 to 200 new sweepstakes are added daily. Also, check out their Winners Circle where members post about their latest wins every day.

A free membership is required to submit your own sweepstakes to their directory.

There is a Monday-Friday free e-newsletter available to members. They include: summaries of the latest sweepstakes news and the top sweepstakes. Subscribers to the newsletter are automatically entered to win a monthly $100 Amazon gift card. Facebook users can also visit their fan page where they also have exclusive giveaways for fans. www.facebook.com/SweepstakesAdvantage.

There is a premium version of the site called Sweepstakes Plus. A small fee grants you access to other features like Expiring and Expired Sweepstakes, Custom My Sweepstakes and Personal Sweepstakes, where you can add your Own Private Sweepstakes and Manage Them in Custom Categories. There are also exclusive giveaways for Plus Members Only.

SweepstakesFanatics   A

www.sweepstakesfanatics.com

Todd Schwartzfarb created SweepstakesFanatics in 2012 because he is an internet marketer who was fascinated with sweepstakes. He started the blog to share his passion with the world. Interestingly enough Todd himself is not

70

a sweeper although he will enter the occasional promotion when he really wants the prize.

SweepstakesFanatics features a free daily newsletter, allows you to search by prize type, and differs in the feature to search by expiration date not entry limit.

Sweepstakes Today A

www.sweepstakestoday.com

Craig McDaniel picked up sweeping as a hobby after he underwent major surgery and had to give up a few of his favorite activities. He started entering online in 1999 after running a search for "sweepstakes" in a search engine. Craig (aka Mr. Sweepy) started Sweepstakes Today in 2004 after winning several major sweepstakes.

Sweepstakes are sorted into various categories including: Featured Sweepstakes, New Sweepstakes and Sponsor's Special Sweeps. You can also save your favorites on My Lucky List. There is a section for freebies and coupons too.

Membership is free, giving you access to the website, the forum and a monthly e-newsletter is sent to all members.

TIP: Keep a small notebook by your computer to write notes, codes and UPCs for current contests and future reference.

Sweeties Sweeps A

www.sweetiessweeps.com

In 1993, when Wendy was a member of a local coupon club, a friend introduced her to sweepstakes. She won her first prize from Captain Crunch that year by sending in six postcard through the mail. Wendy consistently wins prizes every year and has had the chance to go on many adventures because of sweepstakes hobby.

In 2008 she launched Sweeties Sweeps to teach others how to win and share her passion for the hobby. Sweeties Sweeps is free to use. Wendy also offers free sweepstakes courses. In *Sweeping 101* you will learn the basics of sweeping and in *Social Sweeping 101* you learn how to win on Twitter, Facebook, Instagram and Pinterest. In 2009, Wendy launched Sweeties Secret Sweeps a subscription-based site where members find local sweepstakes that are organized by state.

Groups

I became a member of icanwin in Yahoo Groups shortly after I became serious about contesting. I must give credit to the group for helping me by posting contests, answers, UPCs and answers to my many questions as I went from beginner to advanced contestor. I would not have been able to enter as many contests as I have without the group, and the basis of my system started here.

Browser groups are no longer popular as most contest groups are now found on Facebook. Although you cannot search for sweepstakes groups on Facebook, you ask what groups your friends are members of and request to join. Many sweepstakes clubs also have their own Facebook groups to stay in touch in between meetings.

TIP: Be sure to select--Notifications, All--from the Facebook groups so you do not miss any posts, messages or winning opportunities. You can also use Get Notifications or See First from any of your favorite sponsor's pages for the same reason.

Blogs

There are two types of blogs that post sweepstakes: giveaway blogs and influencer blogs. A giveaway blog is similar to a sweepstakes aggregate in that their blog's focus is contests.

There are too many influencer blogs to list in this book. They were originally known as mommy bloggers, but the scope has grown and now includes; dads (parents), chefs (foodies), travel buffs, music aficionados, movie and celebrity reviewers, etc. They almost always host giveaways catering to their readership and followers. If you have a special interest, be sure to follow influencers that will offer giveaways you want to win.

When blogs first started holding contests on their sites they would ask entrants to complete a wide variety of tasks and leave a comment for each action. It was awkward and cumbersome.

In 2011 Rafflecopter created an entry widget and blog contests thrived. Their app made it easier for bloggers to host contests and easier for contestors to enter. Since then other programs have entered the market for bloggers to use; Contest Machine, Giveaway Tab, Gleam and Punch Tab, just to name a few.

Entering a blog contest using one of these programs is very simple. You just follow the instruction(s) on each widget's tabs or pages and you are in to win. Most bloggers add in a variety of ways to garner entries within each widget. They usually involve actions such as; commenting on their blog, visiting their Facebook page or following them on Twitter. Each blogger determines how many entries each action will garner the entrant. Some actions, such as tweeting about the giveaway, may be done each day. (See chapter, How to Win Using Social Media.)

Rafflecopter

www.rafflecopter.com

Greg Goodson, Justin Ratner and J.R.Westbrook created Rafflecopter in 2011. Originally they were working on an e-commerce widget for bloggers when they discovered running blog contests needed a better management system.

There are three levels of service: Free, Blogger and Business, allowing bloggers to customize the widget to both their budget and blog needs. Features include: ease of use, integration with social media outlets and integration with email lists.

Rafflecopter is always evolving. In the future you will see more social platforms, user customization, templates and a custom CSS for more advanced users. They also appreciate feedback so they can continue to grow and improve their program.

They even have a Learning Center to help bloggers and marketers get the most from their giveaways: http://learn.rafflecopter.com/

STORY: Through writing this book I met many women like Carol (owner of This N' That Sweepstakes Newsletter). It never ceases to amaze me how this hobby can touch all aspects of one's life in such a positive way.

የ የ

Carol—Croydon, PA
The earliest I can remember entering sweepstakes was when I was a teen around 1968. My sister and I had entered a radio contest where we had to hand print the words "Kissin' Cousins" as many times as we could on a U.S. Post Card. The prize was a set of movie tickets to see Elvis Presley's new movie Kissin' Cousins and a record album with the music from the movie. My sister had the tiniest printing I ever saw and won the prize. We gathered a group of our friends and all walked the 3 miles from Pennsylvania over to Trenton, New Jersey to see the movie and shop for the afternoon.

I casually entered since then from entry forms I found in magazines, cereal boxes and store drop boxes. In 1977 when I was off on maternity leave with my first child, I began entering pretty regularly and one day saw a stamp in the Publishers Clearing House mailing to order a subscription to Contest Newsletter. I ordered it and was hooked after that!!

I don't remember where I found the rest of the newsletters that I started subscribing to, but it quickly went up to six, if not more, that I was receiving at a time. In those days they were all mail-ins and I entered a lot. I believe my very first win as an "addicted sweeper" was an autographed picture of Roger Staubach, then quarterback for the Dallas Cowboys, thanks to Contest Newsletter. Although many of the original newsletters have gone by the wayside, either ceasing publication completely or merging with other newsletters, I am always to this day on the prowl for new and exciting newsletters and books on sweeping.

In the beginning I did not keep win notices, but I do have four 3-ring binders with the earliest win notice going back to 1978. I did get sloppy at times over the years and did not save all of my win notices so some of them are missing.

I had been hand decorating my envelopes for my own use by using colored markers and stickers. Then around 2002 I started making new designs on the computer. In 2004 I joined my very first sweeping club. I would take my decorated envelopes to the meetings and use them in the envelope exchange. Some of my friends wanted to buy them and that is how my first sweepstakes business, ANN-Tics by Carol, got started.

When the online method of entering began to overtake hand-printed entries, I decided to slow down mailing in entries and began entering online. Around the same time I stopped decorating my envelopes I became a member of This N' That Sweepstakes Stuff newsletter. After my envelope business closed I missed giving back to the sweeping community. It's why I decided to take over the newsletter when the original founder and editor retired. I renamed it This N' That Sweepstakes Club, as I feel it connects all the subscribers together. *(See section, Newsetters.)*

I would like to close with how this hobby has changed my life in wonderful ways I never could have imagined.

ଛଔଓଃ

CELLPHONE

Texting (aka Text Messaging or TXT) or SMS (Short Message Service) on your cell phone is a great way to enter sweepstakes on-the-go. If you have not begun entering via your cell phone, you should start. In the past, contestors used to fill out 3x5 cards and address envelopes while waiting for appointments, for a train, etc. Now you can use that time to enter text contests (or social media ones, see chapter, How to Win Using Social Media).

There are two types of text sweepstakes: ones that are only entered via your cellphone, and ones that have a text entry component to them.

Always read the rules of every sweepstakes to see what the different entry methods are. If text messaging is an option, use it—if the only method of entry is via your cell phone, the odds of winning are the best of all the sweepstakes entry methods at this time, and if it is a component of a sweepstakes, it will usually garner you extra entries into the sweepstakes.

You will be asked to text a specific word, or phrase, to a word representing the company (PIZZA = 74992) or a short code. A fictitious example would be "text WIN to short code 123456".

NOTE: If you are one of the few people that still have a flip phone or a BlackBerry, you will have to know what numbers the word's letters transpose to, as the numbering and lettering will not match on the keypad.

Most mobile phone packages offered by cell service providers come with text messaging packages bundled with the basic phone plan. If by chance you do not have a text messaging package on your phone, you may wish to consider adding a package.

In general, sweepers who do not have a messaging package with their wireless provider are afraid to enter because each message could cost 25¢, 50¢ or more. Yet, those same people will mail off dozens of entries into a promotion paying more in postage, not including the cost of the envelope!

*NOTE: If you see the words **premium message**, enter cautiously. These text sweepstakes cost anywhere from $1 to $5 and the fee will not be absorbed by your text messaging package today. You will be charged the premium message fee each and every time you enter.*

Since each mobile phone is different, I suggest you read the manual for specific instructions on how to use your phone's messaging service.

STORY: I met Rick at one of my Canadian book signings. He told me he had used up all of his luck when he married his lovely wife. I told him it just confirmed he was lucky and to let me know when he won his first grand prize. It only took him six months to win a "big one"..

ॐ

Rick—Pickering, ON

I am fairly new to sweeping and I had been trying all of the different types of sweepstakes I came across. I thought I would try the text message sweepstakes and I stopped by my cellular provider to get a basic text message plan. Armed with 100 text messages per month I started to enter sweepstakes with my cell phone. After the first month of entries, the $85 text message bill and shocked comments from my wife confirmed that I needed the unlimited text message plan.

After upgrading my account, Carolyn told me about a Molson's sweepstakes to "Win the Twins." I started to send the text message faithfully every day until the end of the sweepstakes. One day I checked a voice mail message and was stunned when the voice suggested that I was a grand prize winner. All I needed to do was contact them before a specific date. They administered the skill testing question and confirmed that I did indeed win the grand prize. I had won the "Twins": two brand new Harley Davidson motorcycles!

This was my first large grand prize win. I was surprised but there they were, two shiny new "Hogs." Needless to say, my wife no longer has any issue with my text message bill.

೫೦೧೩

Future Text

This is a cellphone app and can be found in either: the Google Play or Apple App Store. They do not have a website.

Future Text is a text message scheduling service that allows you to preschedule texts. This is a handy tool as it allows you to schedule daily or weekly texts allowing to maximize your odds of entering. The secret is their repitition feature.

It doesn't auto-send texts for you. You still have to open the app and hit send, but it does make it easier to get all your entries in.

Future Text is a freemium app and is supported by advertising. If you do not like ads or want to support future app development, purchase the app.

NOTE: There are several apps that offer similar a service as Future Text. Check your phone's app store for current options and see what works best for you.

*"I'm a great believer in luck,
and I find the harder I work
the more I have of it."*
Thomas Jefferson

ENTERING ONLINE

Entering online, or via the Internet, is becoming the most common way to enter sweepstakes. In the 1950s, judged contests were the most common type of promotion; to reduce administration costs, companies gradually shifted to sponsoring mail-in sweepstakes. Technology has moved forward over the past several decades, and personal computers and smartphones have now become more common than television in most households. Administration costs is also the reason that companies have shifted from mail-in sweepstakes to sponsoring online sweepstakes. Internet and mobile sweepstakes are easier to run and less expensive to set up than mail-in contests; they are also easier and less expensive for people to enter; meaning the company running the sweepstakes will probably receive more entries.

In Canada, mail-in sweepstakes are few and far between. Most of my entries are online. A few are in-person, some are call-in, a smattering of mail-in and heaps of mobile/social media. Companies in the United States are also creating more and more Internet and mobile-based promotions; they see a substantial cost savings by running sweepstakes online as well as a greater interaction with their customers. (See section, Consumer Generated Media and chapter, How to Win Using Social Media.)

The prizes and experiences you can win from Internet-based sweepstakes are as varied as the sweepstakes themselves. To date, 90% of my wins are from online promotions. I have won everything from CDs, DVDs, movie passes, theatre tickets, t-shirts and baseball hats, to a year's supply of bubble gum and fish shaped crackers, a set of cookware, running shoes and many vacations. The list is endless as, on average, I win 5-15+ prizes every month. Basically, anything you could win from mail-in sweepstakes in the past, you can now win online.

My family didn't believe it was a *real* hobby until I won an online contest sponsored by a poultry company. They had an early bird draw (pardon the pun) and my then-husband won. It was a weekend at the Molson Indy car race in gold grandstand seats, all the chicken he could eat, free t-shirts and hats, plus a hot lap around the track in a pace car. Craig got to drive down Lakeshore Boulevard (in Toronto) at 190 MPH! This was a great win for him because he is a huge race fan. After that, everytime he found a giveaway he made sure I was entering! (I also wasn't allowed to serve chicken for a month.)

My favorite prizes are what marketers call experiential prizes. I have met many famous people, but my favorites are: Michael Bublé and Sting.

When I began entering sweepstakes online, I would enter every form manually. It was very time consuming. When I say time consuming, I mean I spent about six-eight hours per day entering sweepstakes.

Since I was unemployed when I started entering sweepstakes on a daily basis, I had the luxury of spending hours manually typing out my information into entry form after entry form.

There was also no rhyme or reason to how I tracked the sweepstakes I was entering. Over time I discovered I was making all sorts of mistakes: entering expired sweeps, entering more than once in one entry only sweeps, not entering daily sweepstakes as often as I was allowed, and I am sure I also unwittingly disqualified myself from dozens of promotions. As I learned what I was doing wrong, I knew I had to come up with a system to track the sweepstakes I was entering, when they ended and who in the household could enter. I also really needed a method to enter each promotion faster. These two needs—the need to track my entries and the need for a system of entering that didn't take literally my whole day—are what lead me to develop the Internet entry system I describe in this book.

Entering online has two components to it: the software tools and the way you can use those tools to your advantage. I will first discuss and describe the tools, then take you through my step-by-step online entry system.

My Online Winning System was created, adjusted, and expanded to its current format over a 10+ year period. It has changed over time because new technologies have emerged and new software packages have been introduced. I also utilized my extensive marketing background and integrated tips and tricks I receive from fellow sweepers. (See chapter, Join a Sweepstakes Club.) As I stated before, experiment and have fun!

"Use all the tools available to you."
W. Clement Stone

SOFTWARE FOR ENTERING ONLINE

Soon after I started sweeping, I noticed people in various online groups chatting about RoboForm Everywhere, an auto-form filling software package. At first I hesitated to use it because I was afraid if I used form-filling software my entry would be disqualified. Sometimes sweepstakes rules state that if you are found to have used an automated sweepstakes entry service you would be disqualified. A paid sweepstakes entry service is very different from auto-form filling software. (See section, Is This Legal?) I also had a fairly slow computer without much memory, and adding another program just might have crashed my system.

By December of 2002, it had become apparent my computer had even become too slow to run our business. So, I broke down and bought a new computer and wow, was it fast! I could get through my sweepstakes in much less time. I started thinking about the auto-form filling software again. I emailed a few people in my online group and was assured using a form-filler would in no way would disqualify me, so I downloaded RoboForm Everywhere. It cut my sweeping time in half! I was hooked.

NOTE: As with any new software package, integrating form filling software into your daily routine does take time to set-up and to adapt to the intricacies of the package. At first, it may seem to be slower. Be patient during this process—it will pay off many times over.

In 2005 I found another timesaving software package: RoboForm Companion. It used the Passcards in RoboForm Everywhere to auto-enter form based sweepstakes. It was recommended to me by a fellow sweeper. He found it very useful, so I thought I would give it a try. WOW! Again, my sweeping time was cut in half.

NOTE: I used RoboForm Companion until 2009 when technology moved so far forward it no longer worked. Since then I have concluded it was an auto-entry system, rather than auto-fill and against contest rules. (See section, Is This Legal? for further details.)

Other sweepers used to love using Sweep and Sweepstakes Tracker because of their ability to track sweepstakes entries. Now many aggregates track also your entries online as one of their website features.

NOTE: Sweep is old and is only available as a legacy download here: http://bit.ly/WavgetSweep

Tracking electronically can be especially helpful if the promotion is one entry per person or household for the entire entry period. Most sweepstakes will disqualify you for duplicate entries and many promotions do not use Repeat Entry Blocks which prevent you from entering twice. Some sweepers prefer using the entry tracking systems offered on several sweepstakes websites. (See section, Aggregates for details about each site and their features.) The benefit of using a Web-based system is, if you travel and do not have a laptop, like to enter from multiple computers, or your tablet, you always have access to your sweepstakes wherever you can access the Internet.

As I have mentioned before, I have based my system around RoboForm Everywhere, but don't take this as my saying that these programs are better than other entry systems or methodologies—experiment, try different programs and packages for yourself, and determine which approach you like best. Remember: **make this hobby your own.** The important thing is to take advantage of computers to do what they do best: doing the same thing exactly the same way over and over again really really fast. Let them do the tedious repetitive tasks so you can concentrate on the important part: entering more sweepstakes!

To maximize the number of entries you can submit on any given day, I recommend you use one or more time saving software packages. It was through talking to others and taking advantage of free trial offers that I came to know about and love the various sweeping tools I currently use. All software packages can be removed from your computer if you do not find them useful.

As time, technologies and entry methods have evolved I now only spend an hour or two per day entering online and on my cellphone. I do not enter as many sweepstakes per month as I did in the past, but I do win as much as I always have. Entering consistently will garner you prizes consistently.

Is This Legal?

The sweepstakes rules usually state an automated entry is illegal. My original fear was that form filling software would be considered an automated entry and I would be disqualified. This is not the case because you are entering the sweepstakes from your computer. The system cannot tell if you manually typed in your personal information or a form filler did it for you. All it does is save your fingers from retyping the same data over and over again.

A company can detect if you are using form filling software only if they enable the database to log time-related information. If they choose to check they would be looking at your IP address, how much time you spent on the entry page and how much time passes between multiple entries from the same address (e.g. spouse, son, daughter, best friend, etc.) not each keystroke on the webpage.

NOTE: IP address stands for Internet Protocol address and is a unique address/numeric code that certain electronic devices currently use in order to identify and communicate with each other on a computer network utilizing the Internet Protocol standard.

It is up to the sponsor to determine the parameters of disqualification. Some companies do not care how you enter, as long as you do, and others write a very detailed clause in the rules about automated entries and the respective penalties. Again, it is very important to read the rules and look for such clauses.

In any case, what most sweepstakes companies are concerned about isn't whether or not you use software to enter your entry information for you; what they are concerned about is whether you have hired a sweepstakes entry service to enter promotions for you using their automated entry systems. Sweepstakes sponsors do not like automated entries because it defeats the purpose of their promotion which is to get you excited about their product or service by participating in their sweepstakes yourself. Paying an automated entry system company to enter for you is completely different, in that you may never see the promotion or even know which sweepstakes you are entering with those services.

NOTE: Using My Online Winning System (or a similar one) will allow you to 1) enjoy the hobby of sweeping and 2) enter you into far more promotions than a service can provide. I average 3000+ entries per month as opposed to the 1000+ offered by many automated entry system companies.

Sweeping Software

Until 2006, there was no form filling software packages on the market for Mac users. Sweepers entering on Macs had to either fill in every form manually or use the AutoFILL or auto-complete feature (usually included with the Internet browser). Now most sweeping software packages work across multiple platforms and devices.

Most of these packages offer a free trial period. If you like a package, buy it. Buying a software package you like and use every day is worth every penny. I believe it is good karma to support the software developers if the package helps you. (See chapter, Attracting Luck.) It will also encourage them to design and create newer and more innovative software to keep up with ever evolving sweepstakes entry forms. Support those who make good tools, and they will support you back.

NOTE: All software packages listed were available at the time of printing; however, some have not been regularly updated. Check www.contestqueen.com for software updates and new programs available.

1Password

http://1Password.com

1Password started out as a password manager and secure wallet for Mac and has evolved to include iOS, Windows, and Android.

If you have a little notebook full of passwords, 1Password is a secure electronic replacement saving you from using weak passwords, password reuse, or the one I find sweepers suffer from the most, PML (Password Memory Loss). It creates strong, unique passwords for all your accounts and logs you in with a single click.

1Password works directly with your favorite browsers, including Chrome, Safari, and Firefox (Mac and PC), Internet Explorer (PC), and Safari on iPhone and iPad. The 1Password browser extension securely keeps all your Logins, Identities, and Credit Cards at your fingertips so you can log in, fill long registration forms or shop online.

For our multi-device world, 1Password can sync your vault of data between all your devices with Dropbox. iCloud sync is an option on Apple devices, as is Wi-Fi Sync if you don't want your data leaving your network. Or you don't need to sync at all—it's your choice.

1Password offers free trial versions of their software at http://1pw.ca/try.

RoboForm Everywhere

http://bit.ly/RFsavings

NOTE: The above URL is a special 60% off your first year offer from Siber Systems for my readers.

RoboForm Everywhere is a password manager and a form filler software package. It completely automates the password entering and form filling process. It does this by allowing you to add Identities with all of the data usually found on online entry forms (such as Name, Address, Telephone Number, Birth Date, etc.). When you open a webpage that has a form,

82

RoboForm Everywhere can fill when you select the Identity you wish to use from the Toolbar and fill the form with one click.

If a form has many more fields, such as a short survey, you can fill in the entire page and save it as a Passcard; every time you return to that particular webpage, you can fill the whole entry with just one click. Passcards also memorize the URL of the form that you have filled. This allows you to use the Logins toolbar command or the Go Fill or Go To in the Passcard Editor to navigate your browser to that web page with the sweepstakes entry form and automatically fill the form from the Passcard.

RoboForm Everywhere runs on multiple platforms: PC and Mac, along with multiple devices: desktops, laptops, netbooks, tablets and mobile phones.

RoboForm Everywhere works on most pages except those built with Flash. It can be used to save those types of pages for sweepstakes entry. It can also be used to speed-up the data entry of forms that have verification codes, are part of a two-step entry process or have multiple frames on the page. (See section, Using a Form Filler to Enter.)

RoboForm Everywhere offers free online tutorials for you to get familiar with their software at http://www.roboform.com/tutorials.

NOTE: The free version of RoboForm Everywhere will only allow you to have ten Passcards. I have more than an average of 150+ Passcards and 300+ passwords I use at any given time. It is worth the small monetary investment in your hobby, just like stamps or Internet access.

NOTE: Sweep or Sweepstakes Tracker are similar software packages. The one difference is that Sweep runs over a standard web browser like Internet Explorer, whereas Sweepstakes Tracker has its own integrated web browser.

Sweepstakes Tracker

www.sweepstakestracker.com

Sweepstakes Tracker is an organizer for handling all aspects of sweepstaking, including online and mail-in entries, your wins and your expenses. Sweepstakes Tracker handles an unlimited number of sweepstakes with an unlimited number of entrants per sweepstakes. With each sweepstakes, you can specify the entry frequency (such as once, daily, weekly, monthly, quarterly and yearly). It also tracks the number of entries in a sweepstakes and the date of your last entry, plus it automatically reminds you the next time an entry is needed in a sweepstakes. It can be configured for manual or automated entry with automatic form filling.

Sweepstakes Tracker has powerful sorting, filtering and data grouping capabilities to view your sweepstakes, along with customizable layouts allowing you to easily switch between views. Also, user definable categories for sweepstakes, wins and expenses allow you to organize their sweepstakes in any way you wish. These features are extremely helpful if you have a large number of sweepstakes. Additional features include an integrated calendar and web browser.

Finally, Sweepstakes Tracker allows you to record all your wins and expenses. A graphical view of your expenses and wins per category is available plus you can export the information to external programs. This feature is very helpful at tax time. (See chapter, Tax Implications.)

Sweepstakes Tracker is available either as a six month subscription for $40 or as an annual subscription for $65.

NOTE: RoboForm Everywhere also works within Sweepstakes Tracker if you do not wish to use their Entrants feature or if you want to use Passcards.

Posting to Groups

https://bitly.com/

This is a very handy website/tool for sweepers. Although most sites auto-shorten links, Bit.ly allows you to take a very long URL, shorten it down and or personalize it. You would want to use this site when posting messages to online groups because sometimes a URL may become unclickable when it "wraps" within the message. This saves others viewing the message from having to cut and paste the URL in their browser or figuring out another way to get to the entry page. It will also save you time when others do the same for you.

EXAMPLE:
Before:
http://www.contestqueen.com/pdfs/news/carolyn/20140710_help_me_boost_my_luck.pdf

After:
http://bit.ly/1rJ2K3L or http://bit.ly/boostmyluck

*"Luck is what happens when
preparation meets opportunity."*
Seneca

MY ONLINE
WINNING SYSTEM

The secret to any system is consistency. I enter sweepstakes every day, 7 days per week. Remember: to win prizes on a consistent basis, you need to enter on a consistent basis. There are days I don't enter any sweepstakes due to a busy life, but I always make sure I go back to sweeping as soon as possible if I do miss a day, or two.

TIP: I recommend entering 1-2 hours per day. That's enough to win plenty, but not so much you cut into work, family time, and any other obligations. Winning should always remain a hobby and not reduce the quality of your life.

On average it takes about 90 days before you begin to win because the sweepstakes you enter today will not be drawn for a few weeks. Don't let this potential lag discourage you—keep entering, and the wins will come. Also, you could enter an instant win sweepstakes online and win TODAY!

TIP: You can find inexpensive computer classes at your local library or community center.

Each step in the online entry system is designed to build one on top of another. That way as you get more comfortable entering online the learning curve required to make an addition or change will be shortened.

NOTE FOR MAC USERS: The Online Winning System is almost the same. The software for Macs is called 1Password, (See section, Sweeping Software.) but the techniques of finding sweepstakes, entering them efficiently, and tracking your entries is the same as for Windows users. You can also use RoboForm Everywhere, but it doesn't work the exactly same on Macs as it does on PCs.

Firstly, ensure you have an email account that you only use on sweepstakes entry forms. You can either set one up with your Internet service provider or you can use a free web-based service (e.g. Yahoo or Gmail). Since more and

85

more websites are requiring passwords with at least one capital letter and one number, create your password for sweeping containing one of each type of character from the beginning. Use the same username and 6+ character password for all your online sweepstakes entries at this beginning level. As you integrate software you will see that they have the ability to generate and save stronger unique passwords.

TIP: You can also use RoboForm Everywhere or 1Password generate and save secure passwords for you saving time. BONUS: I love this feature for all websites I am a member of, not just sweepstakes.

For security reasons, never use the same username or password for personal or business use—that way, if someone gets your sweeping username and password, they can't also use it to access your bank accounts.

Using Your Internet Browser to Enter

When I started sweeping online, I originally began by just saving the online sweepstakes I came across into a folder called Sweepstakes under Favorites in my online browser Microsoft Internet Explorer® (IE). I now use Mozilla Firefox® as my browser of choice and occasionally Google Chrome® if a contest doesn't work in Firefox, as Internet Explorer has too many security vulnerabilities.

NOTE: The system I outline in this chapter is based on Firefox. If you choose to use another browser, the process will be the same, but the specific steps you will take may vary.

As I stated previously, as my list of sweepstakes to enter grew, I began to get confused as to when a contest ended and how many people in the house could enter. I found myself making mistakes, such as entering a giveaway that had already closed. That is how my folder system began.

I created three folders with obvious names:

- Daily
- Weekly
- Monthly

As I found new sweepstakes I would go to the entry page and read the rules to determine end date, number of entries per household and the entry period. I would then save the URL to the appropriate folder with the end date, a new name, and the number of people I could enter.

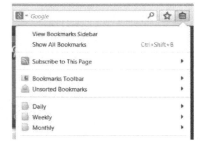

NOTE: I enter One Time Entry Only sweepstakes as soon as I find them and forget about them. You can set up a "One Time Entry" folder if you elect to enter those sweepstakes later in the entry period or you wish to use it to remember which ones you have already entered.

TIP: Enter Daily sweepstakes every day, Weekly sweepstakes on a specific day of the week such as every Monday, and Monthly and One Time Only sweepstakes on the first and/or the fifteenth of the month. That way you will always remember when to enter.

Let me review the system in more detail. Have your three (or four) folders set-up in your Bookmarks before you begin saving sweepstakes links and bring them to the top of your list. I will use a non-sweepstakes site for this example as real sweepstakes sites can change on a daily basis.

For example, you are watching TV, reading a magazine, receive a link via email or see a social media post advertising a sweepstakes whose grand prize is a trip around the world. You decide to check out the sweepstakes and type the sweepstakes URL into your web browser, www.contestqueen.com.

The **first thing** you do is **read the official rules**. There are several things you are scanning for:

- the sweepstakes entry period (e.g. June 1, 2016 to September 30, 2016);
- the region the sweepstakes is open to (e.g. open to all residents of the United States and Canada);
- age restrictions (e.g. persons who are the age of majority or more within the state or province in which they reside);
- how many people per household can enter (e.g. one entry per person or email address);
- how often you can enter (e.g. once per day, once per week, etc.);
- any other requirements or restrictions specific to that sweepstakes.

If you do not meet all of the sweepstakes requirements, even if your name is drawn you will not win. I cannot stress the importance of this enough—I have disqualified myself many times in the past because I rushed reading the rules.

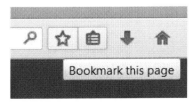

Once you have determined the sweepstakes criteria, save the link in the appropriate folder. For our example, suppose the sweepstakes is running from June 1, 2016 until September 30, 2016, is open to all residents of the United States and Canada who are the age of majority or more in the state or province in which they reside, and allows one entry per household per 24 hour period.

CLICK on the STAR and the page is saved to Bookmarks. CLICK the BOOKMARKS icon to the right of the star. CLICK on UNSORTED BOOKMARKS, hover your mouse pointer over the contest you wish to rename and RIGHT CLICK. A dropdown menu will appear. CLICK on PROPERTIES.

TYPE in the NAME FIELD the end date of the sweepstakes (YY-MM-DD format) followed by sweepstakes name (or something else you will remember such as the prize), and if needed, the number of entrants; **16-09-30 Around the World Trip 1PH.** CLICK SAVE.

NOTE: 1PP equals one entry per person and 1PH equals one entry per household.

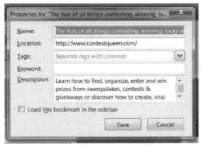

CLICK on UNSORTED BOOKMARKS, hover over the newly named sweepstakes, DRAG it over the appropriate folder. In this case it would be DAILY. You can manually move it into date order or use the sort feature in your browser. The sweepstakes ending the soonest should/will be at the top.

TIP: Having your sweepstakes in end-date order will allow you to enter those that are ending shortly first. This is important for the days you may not have as much time to sweep as it allows you to maximize the numer of entries you submit into each sweepstakes.

As the sweepstakes end dates arrive, enter the sweepstakes and delete the link on the last day. If you are entering on a consistent basis you will always have an evolving list of sweepstakes to enter. I always have a list that has no less than 50 sweepstakes at any given time—I have had it as large as 200+.

TIP: There are far more contests available to enter at any given time than there is hours in the day. This is especially true in the U.S. Be sure to use your entry time wisely and only enter for prizes you really want to win. It is just as easy to win movie passes as it is a car!

To delete a sweepstakes, use the right mouse button and click on the sweepstakes link you wish to remove. A pop-up menu will appear. Select DELETE.

You can also use the Bookmarks Sidebar to view the entire list. It will appear on the left hand side of your screen. Some people find it easier to use than the dropdown menu. I prefer the dropdown menu as it doesn't shrink my screen viewing area.

Be careful as you cannot retrieve a deleted link. You may be able to restore a page using the periodic back-up from Mozilla. (See Mozilla Support: http://bit.ly/restorebookmarks)

Be aware this entry system does not record what sweepstakes you have entered in the past once it has been erased from your Bookmarks. If you want to track what you have entered, you can use a separate Expired folder, a program like RoboForm, or an aggregate like ContestGirl.

TIP: When reading the rules, also check the TIME the sweepstakes ends. Sometimes, it will end at 11:59am, not 11:59pm, which means you only have until Noon the last day to get your final entry in.

To avoid confusion when entering more than one person into a sweepstakes, always enter everyone in the same order. (e.g. yourself, spouse, sister, brother, daughter, son, best friend, etc.)

All browsers have an auto-fill feature. This feature allows the browsers to fill in your data into a form field, either by beginning to type, or clicking, to get a drop down menu of previous data. http://bit.ly/FirefoxAutofill

Multiple Entry Periods

One aspect of being a sweepstakes marketer is I get to see contests from both sides. I have noticed when a contest has several entry periods, many sweepers forget to comeback. The downside for the entrant is they miss out on possibly winning the grand prize. The downside for the sponsor is lower entries. From their perspective is a less than satisfactory result for their program and will potentially impact future marketing budgets (ie. less contests for you to enter).

89

Here is how to track contests with a gap and remember to go back and enter. First, read the rules and find the contest period entry dates. The number of entry periods will determine the number of Passcards you create. Create one for each <u>continuous</u> entry period.

Remember, I use RoboForm to save, organize and enter sweepstakes, but you can adapt this tip for a Bookmark or Favorite based system.

Let's go back to the Around the World sweepstakes example. Assuming three entry periods, the first save would be for end date of the first period. The next two would be for when the next two entry periods begin. Once they start they are edited to reflect the end date.

Let's say the entry dates are the first two weeks of each month for three consecutive months. January 1st-January 15th, February 1st-February 15th and March 1st-March 15th. Save the Passcards in the appropriate folder based on the entry frequency, either Daily or Weekly.

- 16-01-15 Around the World Trip
- 16-02-01 starts Around the World Trip
- 16-03-01 starts Around the World Trip

This way when February 1st arrives, rename the bookmark: 16-02-15 Around the World Trip, and continue to be in to win. This is important because:

1. you want to maximize your entries in each eligibility period, increasing your odds of winning,
2. you don't want to waste your time trying to enter while the contest is dormant,
3. the sponsor sees a continuous flow of entries across the entire contest they will most likely hold another one.

One Time Only

I like these giveaways the best because the playing field is level as everyone has an equal chance. I may be biased since many of the sweepstakes I have won have been from single entry sweepstakes.

There are two theories to entering these sweepstakes: some people enter as soon as they hear about a sweepstakes and others wait until the sweepstakes has been running for some time. I have tried both in the past and I can't definitively say that I have won more one way or the other. You can decide for yourself which way you prefer to enter since your odds of winning are the same either way.

If you choose to enter sometime during the sweepstakes period create a ONE TIME ONLY folder. Your link saving method is almost the same. The only difference is, after you read the rules and discover what the entry period is, select as many dates as you wish to enter for yourself, your spouse, and other family members or friends using their initials as a marker. So using our example from before, the entry would read **16-09-30 Around the World CRW JUL 1 JPM JUL 15 NPW AUG 1 LLW AUG 15.**

This would enter myself (CRW) on July 1, my best friend (JPM) on July 15, my daughter (NPW) on August 1 and my sister (LLW) on August 15, allowing for various entry time intervals throughout the sweepstakes. After the sweepstakes entry date passes for the first person and they have been entered, erase the first initials and entry date allowing you to properly track and space the entries. This will leave it in the One Time Only folder for the next date, when you will enter the next person in the sweepstakes. (See section, Using a Form Filler to Enter about adding and using multiple Identities in RoboForm Everywhere to speed-up entry process.) It is important to remember to remove the names as you enter various people, so that you do not enter anyone more than once and disqualify them.

NOTE: If you enter family and friends into contests on their behalf, ensure that you have an agreement with them in advance if they win, that they will share the prize with you (e.g. trip for four). I have heard many stories of family members no longer speaking or friendships souring because of something that was supposed to be fun going awry. (See section, Increasing Your Chances.)

Ongoing Sweepstakes

There are websites (aggregates and sponsors) that list current sweepstakes. They are usually split into two categories: Daily or Weekly. If you can enter every day to win a prize I have a folder called EVERYDAY. I put all the links to contests that have daily drawings or have an instant win component.

If it's a contest sponsor you should check frequently as they add new promotions on a regular basis, use a folder titled WEEKLY. Your local radio and television stations are good examples of websites that continuously have ongoing giveaways that you will want to check frequently. The specific websites will vary from city-to-city and state-to-state.

Even though most of us can now watch television stations from across the country via satellite/cable

91

services or listen to any radio station around the world via the Internet, most small prizes are for local events, or must be picked up in person. As a result, it only makes sense to enter locally. In my Weekly folder I have the links to all the major television stations, radio stations and newspapers in my area. Most sweepstakes are one entry only per person so having them in my Weekly folder allows me to easily remember to check these sites weekly.

TIP: If you win from a radio station and, for example, their prize policy is you or any one in your household can only win from them once every 30 days, you can add the date of when you can start entering again to the name. e.g. 16-06-30 WKRP

Using a Form Filler to Enter

Once I got a faster computer I began to add sweepstaking software to speed up entering. I discovered using auto-form filling software cut my sweeping time in half, because I no longer had to fill out every online sweeps entry form manually (i.e. type out my personal contact information over and over and over...)

NOTE: The auto-form filling software package I was introduced to first was RoboForm (now RoboForm Everywhere). It is what I started with and what I continue to use. There are many other programs that can speed up your online entries. (See section, Sweeping Software.)

Once I added RoboForm Everywhere it dramatically sped up the time it took me to fill out an online entry form. What I once entered in eight hours, now only took me four! I was now able to fill out the 200+ online entry forms quickly and accurately.

When you first install RoboForm Everywhere, you will be asked to fill out an Identity. An Identity contains all of the information you need to completely fill a sweepstakes form. When you go to a sweepstakes page with a form, RoboForm Everywhere launches a small pop-up window (or just use the Toolbar, depending on what option you chose during set-up) with a list of all the Identities you have added to the program. It is simply a matter of selecting the Identity and clicking on either FILL or FILL & SUBMIT. You will then see all the personal data for that person auto-fill on the form.

NOTE: If a sweepstakes page opens and the RoboForm Everywhere window does not appear, the form is probably in Flash*. You will need to type all the data in manually for this type of form each and every time for each and every person. More and more companies are using Flash based forms because: 1) the website can be more interactive, 'hipper', etc. and 2) it slows the avid *sweeper down. Flash is also not supported by Apple so those forms may not appear properly on your iPad.*

*Flash is a development environment made by Macromedia (now owned by Adobe, www.adobe.com) for creating web content. It allows developers to add animation and interactive content to a webpage. This matters to us as sweepers because RoboForm Everywhere and other automated form filler applications will not recognize forms that are written in Flash. If the sweepstakes uses a Flash based form, you will have to enter the data manually. Entering online sweepstakes entry forms based in Flash will increase your time spent entering online sweepstakes because you must manually enter all your personal information.

It is important to note the difference between Fill and Fill & Submit. You will use Fill & Submit when the page is a plain ordinary entry form page. You will use Fill when the page is not in Flash, but has a two-step entry process, has an authentication code, verification code (aka CAPTCHA) or is in multiple frames, because if you use Fill & Submit you will get an entry error.

NOTE: CAPTCHA is the acronym for Completely Automated Public Turing test to tell Computers and Humans Apart (http://captchas.net/). Usually they have a picture of a set of letters and/or numbers that have been distorted in some way and you have to type in that set of characters correctly into a text box in order to complete the entry. Humans can still read them because we recognize the shapes of letters and numbers even when they've been modified heavily; computers, on the other hand, cannot recognize them.

Always test an online entry form by using Fill first to ensure the form is filled properly and will submit correctly. Once you are sure your entry will be submitted properly, you can use Fill & Submit on subsequent entries. Some sweepstakes have a pop-up agree-to-the-rules feature and you may not be entering properly if you just use the Fill & Submit feature.

TIP: Ensure you set your browser to allow Pop-ups so you do not miss out on finalizing any part of the entry process. This is especially important for social media promotions as most sharing is done via a pop-up window.

Using RoboForm Everywhere Passcards

This is THE key to My Online Winning System. Not only can RoboForm Everywhere Passcards be used to more easily fill forms with additional entry fields such as a questionnaire, they can also be saved and organized within the program for even faster entering.

The organization system is identical to the one that I originally created in my browser and it gives me access to all my contests (and passwords) on all my devices (laptop, netbook, tablet and cell phone).

The system is similar to the browser-based organizational system outlined in the earlier section; Using an Internet Browser to Enter. You can create the folders you require to match the types of sweepstakes you enter. This strategy is scalable and you can add or delete folders as needed.

If you chose to use the same naming system, RoboForm Everywhere will automatically sort them in ascending order. Letters are sorted A to Z and numbers 1 to 9. You can also use the browser to open and edit the folders to delete expired sweepstakes.

You can start by either manually typing all your contact information into the online form, ensuring that all the fields are filled out accurately, or by clicking Identity within RoboForm Everywhere and then clicking on SAVE. A RoboForm Everywhere window will appear for you to name and save the Passcard.

Using the same example as before, I would save the Passcard in the Daily folder in RoboForm Everywhere as **16-09-30 Around the World Trip CRW**. If you are entering others as well as yourself, add their initials to then end of name. If you are only entering for yourself, the initials at the end are unnecessary. Repeat the process saving subsequent Passcards for all the people you would like to enter in the appropriate folder.

TIP: To get the folders listed in order of importance (to you) in RoboForm Everywhere add a number in front of each name to force the order.

Saving a Contest with a CAPTCHA

This step is identical to saving a Passcard, except you edit the form after saving so it will ignore the CAPTCHA. This will stop the auto-entry feature allowing you to fill the CAPTCHA in manually each time.

This is key to the process. When filling out the contest form fill out the CAPTCHA. If you do not, when you go to edit the form, there will be no field to edit.

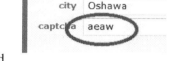

Once you save a Passcard, <u>don't enter the contest</u>. Instead, you are going to edit the Passcard. In the RoboForm Editor click on the Passcard you want to edit. On the far right hand side you will click on the pencil icon. A form will appear allowing you edit the fields you have completed.

Select the CAPTCHA field. Go to the right once again and CLICK on MORE. A drop down menu will appear. CLICK on FIELDS. Another dropdown menu will appear. CLICK on IGNORE FIELD. Then go above and CLICK on SAVE.

Now you can enter the contest using the Passcard. The entire form will be filled as saved and you will be prompted to complete the CAPTCHA. Fill in the current CAPTCHA and enter.

For those contests with weekly answers, such as those from a television show, also use IGNORE FIELD. Replace the '$AnyValueHere$' with the current answer, and add a Login Tip: e.g. new question Wednesdays 10pm. Then enter every day and on the appointed date update the Passcard with the new answer.

Entering with Passcards

Manual Method #1

To enter sweepstakes manually, open RoboForm Everywhere and select LOGINS, EDIT. A new window will open listing every folder and Passcard. Open the manual folder you wish to begin with (e.g. Daily), start at the top of the list and select the first Passcard. Click once. You then have the option to select GO or GO FILL from the toolbar at the top of the screen. If you select

GO, RoboForm Everywhere will take you to the saved page. This is the option to choose for a Flash-based website. If you select GO FILL, RoboForm Everywhere will take you to the saved page and fill all the fields. This is the option to choose if the form has a verification code or two-step entry form that prevents you from entering and submitting automatically. If you click twice (double click) on a Passcard, RoboForm Everywhere will not only GO FILL, but also submit. If there is a verification code, etc. required, you will get an error message.

Manual Method #2
Just as there are many roads to Rome, there is more than one way to use RoboForm to enter manually.

In Firefox select LOGINS, then the folder you want to enter from, such as DAILY, then click each Passcard one-by-one.

If you are using Chrome, you must first select the RoboForm icon in the upper right hand side of the browser bar, and then from the drop down menu follow the above steps.

Semi-Automated Method
To enter sweepstakes semi-manually, similar to Manual Method #1, open RoboForm Everywhere and select LOGINS, EDIT. A new window will open listing every folder and Passcard. Open the manual folder you wish to begin with (e.g. Daily), start at the top of the list, hold down the shift key and select 10 to 25 Passcards. Your options will have changed from GO and GO FILL to BATCH GO and BATCH GO FILL. Click BATCH GO FILL. RoboForm will open the number of tabs equal to the number of Passcards selected in the browser of your choice. Then go to each tab one-by-one, ensure the form is filled out correctly, add in CAPTCHAs required, and then SUBMIT.

*TIP: If a sweepstakes requires a UPC and the entry form is in Flash, you can also add the UPC number right into the Passcard name. For example, for ease of daily entry, you would save the Passcard as; **16-09-30 Trip 0123456789012**.*

Alternative Online Entry Systems

Sweeps, Sweepstakes Tracker and TypeItIn are packages I talk about in this book even though I do not use them as part of my Online Winning System. I believe if I had discovered any of these packages earlier, I may have developed my system around one of them instead of RoboForm Everywhere. Even though I have experimented with different programs and software packages, the others I have tested are very similar to my entry routine and I have felt no need to switch. Try various programs and packages, experiment with various entry methods, find what you like, what is easy for you to use, and have fun!

Remember, hardware and software is ever evolving and so should your online entry system. Never be afraid to experiment with various or new entry methods, programs and software packages to see if a change makes entering easier and/or increases your wins.

Using Auto-Submit Software to Enter

There is a difference between auto-complete and auto-entry. Auto-complete is a feature found within Internet browsers allowing you to more quickly fill out any online form with your contact information. Products like RoboForm Everywhere allow you to auto-fill more complex forms faster by saving all the fields. All auto-complete is done by you on your computer. Auto-entry is when you pay a company to enter contests for you. This used to be done remotely, but sponsors could detect thousands of entries coming from the same IP address, so now those services have migrated to your computer. Regardless of where an auto-entry is generated, it is against the official rules.

I do not recommend you use an auto-entry service or automated submit software because using their services constitutes an automated entry and may disqualify you from most of the promotions you have paid them to enter on your behalf.

The official rules will always have a clause similar to this:

> Sponsor reserves the right, at its sole discretion, to disqualify a person if he/she enters the Contest or tries to do so by any means contrary to these Official Contest Rules or which would be unfair to other entrants or where Contest Entries are generated by any mechanical or automated means. Entry materials that have been tampered with, reproduced, falsified, or altered are void.

Therefore, the use of any automated programs that do not cause a user visible browser visit and a direct user generated submit and are prohibited.

What Happened to RoboForm Companion?

If you purchased the first edition, *You Can't Win If You Don't Enter*, you may recall that I loved an Passcard submission program called RoboForm Companion, by Cydrix Solutions.

A few years later when many computer programs, including Microsoft Windows, updated (technology, hardware and software, is always moving forward) RoboForm Companion did not evolve with it.

I discontinued using it as not only was it giving me errors, but less and less contests were straight entry forms. More and more were using CAPTCHAs, and the shift towards social media giveaways had begun.

As Cydrix Solutions wasn't interested in upgrading their software they sold RoboForm Companion to SweepsU. Originally SweepsU thought they would integrate the program into their website.

Shortly after SweepsU decided they didn't want to integrate an automated entry system into their website. SweepsU shelved RoboForm Companion. SweepsU has since closed and RoboForm Companion went with it.

> *"The best luck of all is the luck*
> *you make for yourself."*
> Douglas Macarthur

Consumer Generated Media

Everything is cyclical. In the 1950s and 1960s most giveaways were judged as an entrant had to complete a jingle in 25-words or less. It's what marketers now refer to as *Consumer Generated Media* (CGM)—also known as User Generated Content (UGC) or social marketing. It is gaining in popularity with sponsors, again, because creating these types of sweepstakes allows them to interact on many levels with their customers. (See chapter, How to Win Using Social Media)

CGM-style sweepstakes ask for the contestant to, for example, create a video, take a picture, write an essay, etc. If you are creative and computer savvy, your odds of winning such a promotion are greater because relatively fewer people will put in the effort to win. That said, if there is a voting component, it may not be the best entry that wins, but the person with the largest network of contacts that garners the most votes. (See chapter, How to Win Using Social Media.) Always read the rules to see how the winner is selected before you put the effort in creating something fun and exciting.

Top Tips on Winning UGC Contests

Walt Arnett has chosen UGC video contests as his preferred method of entry. He doesn't win as frequently as a sweeper, but the prizes tend to be larger. For example, he won this year's Snickers Who Are You When You Are Hungry? Contest, netting the grand prize of $50,000. (You can watch the winning video here: http://bit.ly/SnickersWinningVideo)

Here are Walt's Top 5 Tips:

1. **Show the brand in the best possible light.** What does the brand advertise its best features and benefits are? Ensure you use those in your creation.

2. **Make them laugh.** The reason companies host a contest is it's a fun and engaging way to promote their brand. Therefore, build fun, excitement, jokes, chuckles and laughs into your submission, while at the same time promoting the brand.

3. **Follow the rules.** This is where following the rules is especially important. Rules for a creative contest are more in-depth and have clauses specifically for the entries. Be sure you follow the technical, creative and judging aspects. If you break any clause, your entry will be disqualified.

4. **Use kids and/or dogs.** People love chubby messy cheeks, squeaky voices, wagging tails and furry faces. Kids and animals are also unpredictable adding to the authenticity of the entry. It's why cat videos go viral across the Internet.

5. **Take your time.** Ad agencies do not create a marketing campaign overnight. You shouldn't rush your entry. Think like the sponsor and create an entry they would if they were using it to advertise their brand.

Voting Contests

I am not a fan of voting contests. Most sweepers and every promotional lawyer I work with also detest voting contests. Why? They are notorious for being hacked or hijacked. Entrants either buy votes, cheat or try to get the leaders disqualified. They tend to be very frustrating for the entrants and the sponsors.

Voting contests are popular with companies as they feel it's a great way to get their customers and prospects involved with their product and service. In theory they are a great idea. They get the entrants to engage with the product or service along with viral marketing the giveaway to all their online connections.

Due to the inherent issues with voting contests I recommend you only enter them if:

- there is a random drawing component. e.g. The winner is selected from the top 10 voted.

- it is judged. e.g. The top 10 voted are judged and a winner is selected.
- The number of votes per entry are not shown. e.g. If no one knows who is in the lead, and the entries are randomized, it is harder to dishonestly disqualify the leader.

Protecting Your Entries

Did you know you should protect your pictures online? Especially those you use in photo contests.

Several times in the past several years I have either seen:

- people who have had their personal pictures image stolen and entered into a contest,
- someone using an image taken from the Internet, entered it into a contest and won,
- someone who Photoshopped an image, entered it into a contest and won.

The first way to protect an image is to use selfies, or any image with you in it. It is hard to dispute your face as to ownership to the image, especially if it matches your social media avatars.

The second is to watermark your pictures. There are two free programs you can use:

1. Batch Watermark Photos Online www.watermark-images.com
2. Watermark www.watermark.ws

Here are two examples, one from each program.

It took me three tries of Batch Watermark to get the left image.

I liked the second option much better. You have a lot more control over the watermark and the program didn't alter the image size.

TIP: If you a blogger, there is a program to watermark all your site images: *https://wordpress.org/plugins/image-watermark/*

Does the winning entry look too good? Does it look 'off'? Do you suspect an image has been altered? Use Google Image Search to see if a picture is anywhere else on the Internet. https://images.google.ca/

If you have found one of your pictures used, or suspect an entry has been altered, contact the contest sponsor. Depending on the severity of the infraction submit your complaints as a message or online.

You do not want to come off as a sore loser or a whiny entrant. If contests become a hassle for the sponsors to host, they will stop. You want to come across as their ally in running great promotions, assisting them if things go awry, as they sometimes do in life.

Increasing Your Chances

There are many things you can do to increase your chances of winning. The first being **enter as often** as you are allowed. Read the rules to determine what the entry parameters are: once per household, one time per person, daily, weekly, etc. The entry rules will determine how you proceed. This is especially important if a sweepstakes is labeled "per person" because you can then increase your chances by entering your family and friends.

Entering as often as you can goes hand-in-hand with **entering over the entire sweepstakes entry period**. It is especially important to stagger your entries over the entire entry period when entering via regular mail because it may be financially prohibitive to mail in entries every day.

Look for sweepstakes with **short entry periods**. Sweepstakes that are only open to accepting entries for a two-week period will garner far fewer entries than ones that are open for several months.

Promotions with **entry limitations** attract fewer entrants. I have seen sweepstakes limit entries to a city, a zip code, a state and even specific age ranges.

Look for sweepstakes that offer **many prizes** as opposed to, or in conjunction with, a grand prize. On average, they attract fewer entrants so the odds of winning a prize are higher. Also, some of the best prizes we have won were secondary prizes—hey, even if you don't win the car, a new digital camera is always nice.

Some sweepstakes **take time to enter**. Any sweepstakes with qualifiers; mail-in, essay, video, photo, caption, etc., will draw fewer entrants, therefore increasing your odds of winning.

What are you entering? Enter single entry sweepstakes first, then those with a higher dollar value prize, then instants, then dailies. **Do not waste your time**

101

trolling Facebook for Timeline contests or Twitter for retweet contests. Those you do from your mobile while waiting in line.

Being organized saves time, therefore you can maximize the number of contests you can enter in a shorter period of time. It's why I recommend you use RoboForm and a system to track Daily, Weekly and Monthly contests.

Are you spending enough time entering? If you enter for 30 minutes per day and I enter for 4 hours, my odds of winning are going to be far greater than yours. I recommend entering 1-2 hours per day. That's enough to win well, but not so much you cut into work, family time, and any other obligations. Winning should always remain a hobby and not reduce the quality of your life.

It only takes WON to WIN!
Carolyn Wilman

STORY: This story of how against all odds, in a daily entry sweepstakes, Mary only entered once and WON!

ஐ〇ᘉ

Mary—St. Albert, AB

I couldn't believe my husband and I were going to the Pro Bowl in Hawaii and staying at the Village Hilton! I just wanted to let folks know that even though this sweepstakes could be entered once per day over a four month period, I only entered ONCE. So there you go—keep entering everyone. It only takes one entry. I was also told by the prize authorities the number of entries was approximately 61,000. So, this one was a 1 in 61,000 win!

ஐ〇ᘉ

I also have a story about winning a daily entry contest with one entry. At one point my daily schedule got so busy, as life sometimes does, my entries slowed down to a trickle. One Friday I decided I needed to catch up on all my email. Opening one at a time and take action upon each one. Many e-newsletters had contest links in them. When I went to the Kidding Around Toronto website, I noticed there were several daily entry contests that I had not entered. The one to meet the Barenaked Ladies was ending that day. I thought, *"Darn! I missed the whole thing."* Then I thought, *"What kind of a Contest Queen am I if I am not going to throw at least one entry into the hat. It only takes won to win."* So, I entered myself once and Craig once.

The next night Craig and I had a rare date night. We snuggled on the couch watching a movie. Afterward, he went to his computer to check his email one last time before we went to bed. He discovered a congratulatory email stating he had won the Grand Prize. I danced around the bathroom for a good 15 minutes while I got ready for bed.

We went to their CD signing at Chapters, got an autographed copy of their new CD Snack Time, sat at the front, and an opportunity to take photos with them. I really liked the fine print in the rules: All adults must be accompanied by a child.

Opt-In or Opt-Out?

Many online sweepstakes entry forms have what is known as OPT-IN or OPT-OUT statements.

Example:

☐ **Yes**, I would like to receive occasional, promotional announcements from ACME Inc.

☐ **Yes**, I would like to receive occasional promotional announcements from Judging Agency Inc., the sweepstakes hosting company.

In most cases, if you click on the box, you are opting-in. If you leave it blank, you are opting-out. Be sure to read the text next to each box in case it is reversed.

Companies use these check boxes to create prospect databases—when you opt-in, you are giving your permission for them to send you information at a later date on their products or services. This will result in you receiving email from the company on a regular basis; if you do not want these messages, you should opt-out. However, as the second example shows, many companies offer either advance or start-date notification of new sweepstakes and promotions. If you wish to receive those notifications, you should opt-in. You can always cancel your subscription if you do not like it. Also, the more people that opt-in and the more successful companies feel their sweepstake promotions are, the more sweepstakes they will hold, increasing the number of prizes available.

TIP: Be sure to read the rules, because some promotions require you to opt-in in order to receive an entry into the sweepstakes, while others offer bonus entries.

Remember, there are two schools of thought on this subject and you should decide for yourself which you choose to follow. The first is: to cut down on spam, always opt-out. The second is: if you wish to be notified of sweepstakes and promotions from sites and companies that run them on a regular basis, opt-in.

Time Saving Tips

There are many little things you can do that will save you time entering online:

1. Use the fastest computer you can.
2. Use the fastest Internet connection you can.
3. Use sweeping software packages such as RoboForm Everywhere and/or Sweepstakes Tracker.
4. Have two browser windows or tabs open at once and toggle back and forth between them. This is particularly handy when web pages are slow to load.
5. Only enter sweepstakes with prizes you really want to win.
6. Only enter the people that will share the prize with you, such as your spouse, child, or best friend.
7. Only enter the required fields. They are usually flagged by a * or are bolded or colored.
8. Only enter online. Mail-in sweepstakes take quite a bit of time to enter in comparison to online promotions.

STORY: Rachel relates her tale of how it really does take just as much time to win a car as movie passes. One of the most exciting aspects of this hobby is you never know what you are going to win or when.

୧୦୯୫

Rachel—Morrisville, NC

The answering machine message from the bank left my husband concerned. Call the bank back promptly. Did we bounce a check? Did someone steal his identity? As he talked on the phone I walked in. With a quizzical look on his face he turned to face me, "You won't believe this," he said. "We won a car."

A few months prior, I begged him to drive 30 minutes away to a car rental company that was sponsoring a contest for a car along with our bank. I filled out the entries (one per person) and dropped them in the box. My husband, who was skeptical, remained in the car.

Thus, began my hobby of entering sweepstakes and contests. After the first car win, I reluctantly sent off for some miracle water advertised by a local TV evangelist. Couldn't hurt, I thought. After all, he said he had a special connection with The Almighty!

After receiving my miracle water I followed the directions and asked for a win, a few weeks later I won another car. I never told anyone until recently, because I felt like an idiot. After all, who asks God for a win in a contest!

I didn't use the miracle water again; however, I use four leaf clovers in envelopes I put in the mail. I also like using colored envelopes, stickers, cute stamps, fancy postcards and other fun ways to give me "an edge." I have reaped the rewards by winning many sweepstakes.

Every day I find a new contest or sweepstakes to enter. People think I'm crazy until I tell them what I have won. I enter by mail, online or drop box and will often go out of my way to enter for a trip to Vegas.

Recently, a local contest asked for a story regarding a funny bathroom moment. I submitted a poem about my cell phone dropping in the throne. My win….an upscale toilet with all the latest gizmos! "We couldn't stop laughing," the lady at the other end of the phone said.

∞⊗

Refer Your Friends

Have a circle of sweeping friends—it comes in handy when there are sweepstakes that will grant you bonus entries into the sweeps for referring other people. I have a standard email list of ten specific contesting friends I use.

Many sweepstakes ask for referrals without granting bonus entries. I only enter friend's email addresses in those sweepstakes that grant extra entries. I also only refer the friends I know will enter. Making friends in the sweeping online communities can help because you know they will enter and increase your odds of winning. (See sections, Newsletters, Sweeping Clubs or Aggregates.)

There are two types of referral bonus entries: direct and closed-loop. The direct referral will give you a bonus entry into the sweepstakes, just for referring someone. The closed-loop will only give you a bonus entry if the person you referred returns to the website and enters the promotion. This is usually tracked by an email sent to the referral with a unique URL back to the promotion website.

Entering For Others

Entering your family into contests increases your odds of winning. I used to enter my ex-husband, mom and siblings into contests. I don't any longer due to time constraints, but I still enter my daughter. You can also enter friends, but unless you have an agreement to share the prize, don't.

Some people feel that entering on behalf of others is cheating. I disagree. I have discussed this issue with sponsors and they feel if the rules are followed, entering a spouse, daughter or best friend is fine as it helps them to reach their marketing goals.

Be aware, unless you have someone's social media account login and password, you cannot enter them into Facebook, Twitter, Pinterest or Instagram contests. Same with text-in-to-win. You would need their cellphone or permission.

"You are what you share."
C.W. Leadbeater

HOW TO WIN
USING SOCIAL MEDIA

DICLAIMER: Facebook, Twitter, Instagram and Pinterest have not sponsored or endorsed this book.

Entering sweepstakes on social media platforms are now the majority of the giveaways I enter on a daily basis. Companies have flocked to these platforms for a variety of reasons. It allows them to;

- interact directly with their prospects and customers,
- allows them to viral their message(s) across the Internet and multiple platforms via their followers and fans,
- generally engages their fans and followers for a greater period of time than a standard entry form,
- more easily create Consumer Generated Media (CGM) promotions,
- and, cuts down on cheating as every entrant must have an account on the platform of choice.

"If you are not growing, you are dying."
Unknown

As companies shifted to social media I began to feel the backlash. Sweepers would message me. They were upset their sweepstakes mail-in hobby was disappearing, Not only did contests move online, they were shifting to social media. Emails would resoundingly sound similar to this:

"There are a lot of us out there who signed up to things etc. expecting to be able to enter, or get information and etc. through e-mail. We DO NOT Facebook, Twitter, Blog.... nor do we want to! Why do all these people, companies, or corporations think we do?"

Companies do not care if you are tech savvy, or not. I know this is harsh, but they have marketing and sales objectives they want to meet. If you are not on social media you are most likely not a corporation's target market, so they do not care about you. They care about making money. It's why any and every business is in business. If you choose to not to participate on social mediathen you will eventually be out of a hobby.

I am also a Sweepstakes Strategist. I research the hobby from a marketer's perspective on a daily basis. I read articles, track trends and test new methodologies. The reason companies love social media marketing is that it engages and encourages the entrant to viral their marketing message for them. Companies are seeing a far greater return on their promotional budgets than ever before, therefore instigating them to host more social media giveaways.

With any new skill, be patient with yourself. Learn one social platform at a time. Only when you are comfortable with one, move on to the next. Otherwise you will find yourself overwhelmed. Once you learn the ins and outs of social media and are having fun, you will wonder why you waited so long to start posting, tweeting and regramming.

Are you eligible to win?

When I share giveaways on Facebook, Twitter and Instagram, I often get asked, "Is this open to Canada?" or "Is this open to the USA?" etc. What they are wanting to know is, "Am I eligible to enter?"

All social media contests should have proper rules. Many do in the original giveaway post (on Facebook or Instagram) or with a link (on Twitter or Pinterest) as it's impossible to provide proper entry details in 140 characters.

If you see a contest without a link, one tip is to look at the sponsor's handle. If they have a country in their account name, their promotions will only be open to that country. e.g. @Samsung is the Korean account, @SamsungUSA is the American account, @SamsungCanada is the Canadian account, etc.

In a similar vein, if the company's URL ends in .ca or .uk or .au, the promotion is only open to Canada, the U.K. or Australia.

If you are unsure, send them a message on their wall or feed asking about eligibility and/or a link to the rules. The sponsor doesn't want ineligible people entering as it wastes everyone's time so they will respond.

My #1 tip is to *always read the rules*, and in this case, hunt them down first too.

Your Profile

I recommend you complete your profile on every social account you own. It gives your account credibility which is appealing to sponsors. They do not want to be giving away prizes to eggs, color bars or silhouettes.

If you don't want to use a picture of your face, pick something happy and real in your life like your pet, flowers from your garden, your sports car, etc. Cartoons or nothing at all make your account feel fake.

Be sure to complete all areas including the banner, avatar, description, etc. I would avoid putting sweeper, winner, contest, comper, etc. as it may make you appear greedy.

That said, those words are included in all my profiles as I use them for both work and play, but my profiles are written as a business account, not a personal one. I also believe it hinders me and reduces my chance of winning. Legally it shouldn't, but who is to say a marketing manager doesn't like who I am and draws another name.

Platform Changes

The Internet moves so quickly, that in the span of time I started writing this book and finishing it all the social platforms changed and evolved. They changed enough that I had to rewrite some of the sections. Be aware how important it is to learn how to use each social platform well and keep abreast of updates. Be sure to follow me online, and other sweepstakes thought leaders, as we all write about these shifts and how they affect the hobby. You can find the aggregates in the Resources section of my site. (http://contestqueen.com/resources/) Explore each website and sign-up for their newsletter, blog or podcast, etc. Next check all their social feeds to see if what they are posting is of value to you. If it is, Like, Follow, etc. This will ensure you are quickly allerted to all industry changes and can change your winning strategy accordingly.

How to Win on Facebook

NOTE: This section assumes you already have a public Facebook account. If you are new to Facebook, search Google or YouTube using the keywords "how to use Facebook" for online lessons, classes, videos and additional resources.

There are two types of contests on Facebook: giveaways hosted on Facebook and giveaways on the sponsor's Facebook Timeline.

Contests Hosted on Facebook

Until recently companies were not allowed to host a contest on Facebook unless they used a third-party program such as EasyPromos, OfferPop, ShortStack, Strutta, Wildfire and Woobox, just to name a few.

These programs allow a company to create a Facebook sweepstakes, upload it to a TAB allowing their followers to enter to win. These sweepstakes can range from straight entry forms through to advergames. They are not much different than a contest hosted on a sponsor's website or dedicated webpage. The only difference is; you need a Facebook account to enter.

Entering these types of sweepstakes is as varied as "regular" online sweepstakes. Generally you are asked to fill out an entry form with your contact information and you are in to win or you could be asked to play a game, answer a question, upload a picture, etc. You get the idea.

Facebook Timeline Contests

In 2013 Facebook changed its Promotional Guidelines allowing companies to host Timeline contests. So, what does a Timeline contest look like?

I ran a social media contest giving away a $25 gift card to use as an example in this book.

NOTE: My example doesn't follow Facebook's current Promotional Guidelines as Pages are not allowed to ask entrants to share or tag friends. That said, Facebook does not crack down on offenders, as the same companies breaking the rules spend millions buying ads and boosting posts generating income for Facebook.

This is what I posted on Facebook:

I am hosting 3 giveaways!!

Win 1 of 3 $25 gift cards on Facebook.
(You can win 1 on Twitter & 1 on Instagram.)

1) Like this page.
2) Like this picture/post.
3) Tag a friend in the comments.
4) Share this post.
5) One entry per person.
6) Ends March 4th 2015 at 11:59pm ET.
7) Open only to Canadians.

I believed the rules I wrote were simple and clear, yet an extraordinarily amount of entrants didn't follow them. How do I know? Because the numbers don't lie.

If everyone followed the rules, they all would have liked, commented and shared the post and the entry numbers would be equal. They are clearly not. When I selected my potential winner, I checked to see if they followed all the steps.

Thankfully they had, so I didn't need to go to the back-ups I had also drawn.

You must follow all the steps a sponsor posts to be in to win.

The fun doesn't stop there. You may not have ended up in the final drawing at all!

If you have a Facebook account you use for entering sweepstakes and have locked down the privacy settings, sponsors can't copy or count your entry for the final drawing, which means you aren't even in to win.

Check your privacy settings to ensure contest sponsors can see your entries.

So if you are entering Facebook giveaways and you are wondering, "Why am I not winning on Facebook?" or worse, get frustrated and think "I hate Facebook contests. I never win." Here is what you can do to increase your odds of winning.

Do you know if you are even entering? That seems like a silly question. You might be saying, "How could I not even be entered?" Did you enter on the sponsor's original post or on a friend's share?

The #1 mistakes I see when entering Facebook Timeline contests are entrants liking, comments and sharing the wrong post.

What do I mean by that? Many Timeline contests ask you to like, comment and share the contest post.

Here is an example: while scrolling your news feed you spot a giveaway a friend shared on their Timeline.

It asks you to like the post, so you do. Which image did you like? Your friend's share or the sponsor's post?

You must click on the word *photo* to go to sponsor's original post to ensure you like the correct image.

It asks you to leave a comment, so you do. Similar to a like, where did you leave the comment? On your friends shared image or did you go back to the sponsor's page and find the original contest post?

Using the image above as an example, if you click like, share or leave a comment here, you will not be in to win.

It asks you to share. Did you share the giveaway properly?

Firstly, be sure you share it on your own Timeline.

Secondly, be sure the post is public so the sponsor can confirm your entry. This public setting is different than your personal page public setting. If you want to know if your settings are correct, try viewing your own Facebook account as a stranger. Can you see your contest shares? If not you need to make some changes to your settings.

My final winning Facebook tip is: *(cue shameless promotion music here)* Like my Contest Queen Facebook Page as I share tips, tricks, news, and giveaways.

https://www.facebook.com/TheContestQueen

Now that we have discussed sharing Timeline contests, there is a different type of sharing; promotional app giveaway shares.

When you enter a contest hosted by a promotional app , after you submit the entry page, you get a exit page asking you to share the contest on your social channels for additional entries.

TIP: When sharing the promotion on your Facebook wall ensure the share is set to Public or Friends.

Some people are discouraged by referral giveaways, as they don't have many social connections. To make matters wose, some of the apps are notorious for not counting referral entries. My philosophy is; <u>it only takes won to win</u>, so enter anyway.

New Winning Opportunities

If you find a sponsor that consistently hosts sweepstakes on their Facebook Timeline, not only do you want to select ALL ON under Notifications, you also want to ensure you select See First under In Your News Feed. This will ensure everytime to open Facebook, any Page that you have chosen to See First will appear at the top of your newsfeed, no matter when they posted to Facebook.

You can also select to See First any posts from friends or family. This is a handy feature to use with your sweeping buddies so you can enter any new contests they share.

TIP: Do not select See First on too many pages or friends as it will make your news feed unmanageable. You still want to see what other fun and winning oppportunites might come scrolling down your news feed.

How Winners are Notified

The perception is, if you like, tag, share, etc. in Facebook Timeline contests the sponsors have no way to track those entries, other than by counting them one by one. If there are thousands of likes and/or comments, how would anyone properly, randomly select a winner? There's an app for that! If you are a blogger or small business, one of the free tools you can use is Woobox.

If it's a Facebook Timeline contest, the sponsor will either share your name as a winner in another post, or tag you in a comment on the original post. That means you either have to remember to go back to their page, get

notifications, always check your notifications (which you should be doing anyway!) or have awesome sweeping buddies that will let you know they saw your name.

TIP: The notification icon is a little world/globe in the top navigation bar in Facebook.

Even though it's against Facebook's Promotional Guidelines, some companies will try to send you a message in Facebook. If they are not your friend, the message will end up in your secondary inbox called Message Requests. Be sure to check it frequently so you do not miss a single winning notification.

If it's just a contest held on Facebook, similar to an online contest, where you fill out a form, you will either get an email notification or a phone call. No different than a 'regular' sweepstakes.

Another way to find out if you have won on Facebook is to do a search. Type the words *winner [your name]* or *congratulations [your name]* in the Facebok search bar to see if any posts are found.

Playing by the Rules

Many people complain they are not lucky when it comes to winning Facebook contests. Let's look at some reasons as to why you may not be winning.

Public Posts

Company's frequently ask you to LIKE, COMMENT, SHARE or TAG A FRIEND to be in to win a prize. Your share should be public so the sponsor could see the share if they choose to go to your page and look.

One alternative option is to make the post public but to only share it to a list you create of contest friends. That way non-sweeping friends and family will not see it.

Another is to post it to a Facebook group. It can be an open giveaway group or a closed group. My contest club has a closed group that we frequently share to.

A third is to share it privately and hope the sponsor doesn't check your feed and only relies on the share numbers when drawing., which is most likely the case.

Two Accounts

Many people are concerned their friends and family will get fed up with seeing so many contest posts on their feed. It's why many sweepers have two Facebook accounts. One for friends and family and one for entering sweepstakes. However, having two accounts is against Facebook's rules. (Terms of Use: https://www.facebook.com/terms.php)

The second sentence in section four states, "2) You will not create more than one personal account."

Although it's against the rules, I have not met anyone who has had one or both of their accounts shut down. Even though it is within Facebook's legal right to do so.

Having two accounts doesn't effect your odds of winning, directly. As long as you are following the contest rules, you are in to win. How it could affect your odds of winning is, if a promotion gives additional entries for referring your friends and you don't have any, the total number of entries you have in any given sweepstakes will be lower.

Make connecting with sweeping buddies on Facebook a priority when entering on this platform. Ones you can share contests with and who can share with you. I have had the pleasure of making real friends with people I first met online and then met in person at a sweepstakes convention, meeting or workshop.

Breaking the Rules

When companies ask us to SHARE or TAG A FRIEND on their Facebook Timeline contest, they are also breaking Facebook's rules! (Page Guidelines: https://www.facebook.com/page_guidelines.php)

Clause three states, "3. Promotions may be administered on Pages or within apps on Facebook. Personal Timelines and friend connections must not be used to administer promotions (ex: "share on your Timeline to enter" or "share on your friend's Timeline to get additional entries", and "tag your friends in this post to enter" are not permitted)."

So why do so many companies do it? They do it for several reasons:

- They do not know any better.
- They do not care.
- They see other companies breaking the rules and not being punished for it. Why should they stop when they are garnering the social results they are seeking?

Although their requests are against the rules, if you don't follow them, you won't be in to win. It's why I added against policy clauses in my original example. To teach you all aspects of Facebook Timeline contests you will come across.

What should you do about all the 'illegal' Facebook contests you come across?

1) You could do nothing. Just follow the contest rules when you enter and hope you win.
2) You could let the company know they are breaking the rules and should change their marketing practices to fit within the platform's guidelines.
3) You could report them to Facebook. However, it could get the company's Facebook page closed. If every company's page was shut down that broke the rules we would quickly run out of contests.

What is Public?

Many people are afraid to make their Facebook account public for a variety of reasons. Whatever your reason is, be aware, if you find you are not winning, you may wish to alter your settings.

As I use my Facebook account for entering sweepstakes, I generally keep everything public. I don't care that the world can see I entered to win a trip, car, or anything else. Plus, being public, sponsors can easily see my share.

I have known since I got my first email address in 1994 to never put anything 'out there' that you don't want the world to see. Even if I create a post that is a bit personal (e.g. a few late night sad ones as I went through my divorce and needed support) and I only shared it with friends, I make sure they are not too revealing or overly dramatic.

That said, some people want the world to see very little, or nothing. If that is the case, you will need to follow Facebook's guidelines on how to change your account settings. Learn more about the basics of Facebook and their privacy policies on their website: https://www.facebook.com/about/basics

Facebook Jail

Did you know if you Like too many things too quickly you can find yourself in Facebook jail?

This is a problem for contestors because not only are you blocked from Liking or Commenting on anything on Facebook for 7-30 days, everything you have liked for the past 30 days is deleted!

What do you do?!

Nothing. Appeals to Facebook will go unheaded. You have to bide your time and await your release.

What you need to do is rethink your contest entry system and where you are spending your time vs. the dollar value of what you are trying to win. I believe if you do that you will not go back to Facebook jail once released.

Thankfully, I have never been in Facebook jail and believe it's because I do not enter heaps and heaps of Timeline contests in rapid succession. I first focus on big prizes and only if I have time, or have some down time do I enter Timeline contests.

HOW TO WIN ON TWITTER

NOTE: This section assumes you have a public Twitter account. If you are new to Twitter, search Google or YouTube using the keywords "how to use Twitter" for online lessons, classes, videos and additional resources.

Twitter has changed a lot since I first started using it in 2009. Twitter is far easier to use now than it originally was. I chose to start using TweetDeck. It allowed me to figure out the platform faster and connect with others easier. As I got more proficient with Twitter, I moved to Hootsuite as it was a virtual social media manager with the biggest benefit being to schedule tweets.

RESOURCE: Twitter has a fairly simple Getting Started page for you to learn the basics. http://bit.ly/TwitterGetStarted

Contests on Twitter

Just like Facebook, Twitter also boosts two types of contests; contests being run on Twitter and shared links to contests being hosted elsewhere.

There are two types of giveaways you will find being run on Twitter:

- those that are one-offs,
- and those that are held frequently, daily, weekly or monthly.

The one-offs you will only find as you happen to be scrolling through your feed. There is no way to track or organize those types of giveaways. All you do is follow the instructions within the tweet. You will usually be required to follow and/or retweet (RT), or reply with an answer to the tweet, to be in to win.

I recommend you organize the frequently, daily, weekly or monthly exactly the same way you organize all your other contests. For example, there are

117

several companies I know of that hold a contest every week on their Facebook and Twitter accounts. I saved a link to their Twitter page in my Weekly folder with a preface, such as TUE or WED, indicating the day of the week, so I remember to go back. Repeat the process of each type for social media promotion.

Finding Contests on Twitter

Finding giveaways on Twitter (and Instagram) isn't as easy as finding those online or on Facebook. The reasons are:

- they aren't shared on the sweepstakes aggregates as frequently as online, Facebook or blog contests are,
- and they aren't as searchable on Google.

The best ways I have found to find those types of contests are to:

- read all the entry options on contests posted on the aggregate sites. Sometimes Twitter and Instagram is included as an entry option.
- follow sponsors who frequently host giveaways on all platforms.
- follow fellow sweepers who regularly retweet and regram. Ask your online friends for their handles and share yours. (Feel free to follow me on Twitter @ContestQueen or on Instagram @TheContestQueen.)

The specific type of giveaways being held on Twitter fall into three categories: retweet to win, reply to win or quote to win.

You can do searches for the words 'RT & Win' or 'Follow & RT', but I find the results are not always accurate as they pull in any tweet with those words from all over the world. I also create lists so I can quickly scroll through sponsors or friends to find giveaways.

What also worked was searching Twitter with the parameter "US only". It netted a lot of results including: RT to win contests, links to regular contests, Twitter party announcements, etc.

Using Hashtags

A hashtag is a word with the pound sign at the beginning. **#hashtag**

If a contest post includes a hashtag as a requirement of entry, you must use it. If you don't you won't be in to win. Sponsors and agencies use hashtags to track their marketing results. Those same hashtags are plugged into services, programs and apps so they can track promotional results, collect online analytics plus draw the winners.

Who to Follow & Why

The best place to find Twitter contests is to follow fellow sweepers, and then sponsors that regularly host giveaways. You will find:

- Twitter feed contests
- links to giveaways hosted on other platforms,
- Twitter party announcements,
- sweepstakes where you submit your entry via Twitter,
- and 'Follow & RT' contests.

Other ways to find Twitter contests (and these tips also apply to Instagram) are:

- **read all the entry options on sweepstakes posted on the aggregate sites**. Sometimes social platforms are included as an entry option.
- **follow sponsors who frequently host giveaways on all platforms**.
- **follow fellow sweepers who regularly retweet and regram**. Ask your online friends for their handles and share yours

Once you are following sponsors and sweepers, add them to Lists for quick scrolling.

A third way to find Twitter giveaways is to search for currently trending hashtags. New movies do this frequently.

In the Twitter search bar look for giveaways using the sponsor's official movie hashtag. Then you will see what the TOP search results are, followed by the LIVE ones.

To narrow down the results, earch for the giveaway using the sponsor's official hashtag AND add in a parameter such as contest, sweepstakes or a city. Then see what the TOP search results are, followed by the LIVE ones.

Then click on either the contest sponsor's Twitter handle or the embedded link to enter.

Twitter Feed Contests aka Follow & Retweet

I ran a social media contest giving away three $25 gift cards. One on Facebook, one on Twitter and one on Instagram.

This is what I posted on Twitter:

> #Win 1 of 3 gift cards. Follow me & RT this post
> #WinWithTheContestQueen

Out of all three options, this was the easiest way for someone to win a gift card from me. All you had to do was follow me and retweet the image.

If you are new to Twitter, here is what the symbols mean:

- The left pointing arrow is REPLY.
- The two arrows squared is RETWEET.
- The stacked squares is BUFFER. (You may not see this one if you don't have a Buffer account.)
- The star is FAVORITE.
- The graph is TWEET ACTIVITY.
- The three dots are a DROP DOWN LIST with additional options.

TIP: You can see how many times a tweet has been retweeted (bottom left hand corner) to discover what your odds of winning are.

To ensure you are retweeting the correct image, and that the contest hasn't ended, always go to the sponsor's Twitter feed and find the original tweet. Then read the rules, and follow them, to be in to win.

My final winning Twitter tip is: *(cue shameless promotion music here)* follow me as the @ContestQueen on Twitter as I share tips, tricks, news, and giveaways.

How Winners are Notified

Companies will tag a winner with their handle (i.e. @ContestQueen). Anyone that uses your handle in a tweet will appear in your notifications. Notifications also let you know if you have been tagged, liked, retweeted, replied to or mentioned. Check them daily as to not miss any important messages.

Companies may also Direct Message (DM) you. Only people following each other can DM. If a big company suddenly follows you, it may be a very good sign a prize is coming your way.

Creating Lists

Creating lists becomes more important the more people you follow on Twitter. I follow over 1000. My news feed flies by so quickly, sometimes I miss heaps of winning opportunities. The best way to slow down the feed, and narrow down what you see is to create LISTS.

They are completely customizable. You can create anything you wish as there are no limits.

I have 14 lists in categories such as: Media, Celebrities, Contest Buddies, Contest Sponsors, Marketing, etc.

Your Lists are one of the clickable options on your Twitter page.

 If there is an account you follow, and you want to add them to a list, click on the gear icon beside the Follow/Following button.

NOTE: You do not have to be following an account to add them to your list.

Twitter also has an online tutorial on how to create Lists: http://bit.ly/UsingLists. You can also Google "how to create a list in Twitter" and get almost ½ billion results. I am sure one of those can help you!

If you want to see only the feed from a list you created, go to your profile, CLICK on LISTS, then selct the list you want to troll.

Twitter Parties

A Twitter party or chat is a live 30-60 minute conversation usually hosted by a blogger and sponsored by a business, company, product or service. Most give away amazing prizes over the course of a party, so it is worth your time to attend one or two per week.

Just like any other contest, if you are not entering correctly, you won't be in to win. Read the rules and ensure you follow these steps:

RSVP
Some parties require you to RSVP on the sponsor's or lead blogger's page about the party. If you are not on the list and your name is drawn your entry will be disqualified and another name will be selected.

Reply Properly
The standard party format is a series of questions (generally 6-10) related to the sponsor and their current marketing program.

A sample question may look like:

Q1 What is your favorite activitiy to do with your kids when it's warm and sunny outside? #SummerFamilyFun

You will notice the tweet is in the 'standard' party format of:

- the question number,
- the question designed to create a conversation and engagement,
- followed by the event hashtag.

If you do not answer using the REPLY icon on the question tweet to respond/answer, you will not be in to win as the prize for that question is usually drawn from the replies.

Just as important, if you do not use A1 in your response, you will not be in to win as the moderator has no way of knowing what question you are responding to. Twitter parties move fast and the hosts only have moments to verify winners. You have to make it easy for them to know you understand the party requirements for winning.

Use the Party Hashtag
How is anyone to know you are even at the party if you are not using the event hashtag? No one except your followers who will see your tweets. The way moderators and attendees follow everyone in attendance is via the hashtag either directly in Twitter (try searching any hashtag and see what happens) or as a stream in a program such as Hootsuite, TweetDeck or Twubs.

Have Fun
Part of the fun of participating in the party is to engage with fellow attendees and connect. As part of the sweeping community it is nice to see friends online and their answers. Many come up with wonderfully funny quips or adorable pictures I like to share and/or comment on. Remember to always include the hashtag in every one of those posts too!

Notifying Party Winners
The Competition Agency has an app called Tweet Draw. Many party hosts use it as it's a convenient way to select winners.

They can draw from all:

- those who retweeted a specific tweet,
- the followers of a specific account,
- or from a specific hashtag.

Some hosts, use Woobox and others will copy all the people who answered a party question, paste them in a spreadsheet and use Random.org to select a winner.

The host will also tag you in a winner announcement tweet and you will get dozens of congratulatory tweets. You will know you won!! All the mentions of your handle (eg. @ContestQueen) will be found in your notifications.

Twitter Jail

Similar to Facebook, you can also find yourself in jail. The technical limits for Twitter accounts are:

- **Direct messages (daily)**: The limit is 1,000 messages sent per day.
- **Tweets**: 2,400 per day. The daily update limit is further broken down into smaller limits for semi-hourly intervals. Retweets are counted as Tweets.
- **Changes to account email**: Four per hour.
- **Following (daily)**: The technical follow limit is 1,000 per day. Please note that this is a technical account limit only, and there are additional rules prohibiting aggressive following behavior. Details about following limits and prohibited behavior are on the Follow Limits and Best Practices page. https://support.twitter.com/articles/68916#
- **Following (account-based)**: Once an account is following 2,000 other users, additional follow attempts are limited by account-specific ratios. The Follow Limits and Best Practices page has more information.

Thankfully, I have never found myself in Twitter jail. I do not tweet enough, even at Twitter parties, to limit my account.

Twitter Spam

What I love about social media is, it keeps you on your toes because just when you think you have it figured out, the platform changes, updates, changes it's policies, etc. , and you have to adjust. It's like being at an arcade playing the shooting game where the targets move, except in this arcade, the floor keeps moving too!

Here is what Twitter looks at your account to determine if it's 'spammy':

- If you have followed and/or unfollowed large amounts of users in a short time period, particularly by automated means (aggressive following or follower churn);
- If you repeatedly follow and unfollow people, whether to build followers or to garner more attention for your profile;
- If your updates consist mainly of links, and not personal updates;
- If a large number of people are blocking you;

- If a large number of spam complaints have been filed against you;
- If you post duplicate content over multiple accounts or multiple duplicate updates on one account;
- If you post multiple unrelated updates to a topic using #, trending or popular topic, or promoted trend;
- If you send large numbers of duplicate @replies or mentions;
- If you send large numbers of unsolicited @replies or mentions;
- If you add a large number of unrelated users to lists;
- If you repeatedly create false or misleading content;
- Randomly or aggressively following, favoriting or retweeting Tweets;
- If you repeatedly post other users' account information as your own (bio, Tweets, url, etc.);
- If you post misleading links (e.g. affiliate links, links to malware/click jacking pages, etc.);
- Creating misleading accounts or account interactions;
- Selling or purchasing account interactions (such as selling or purchasing followers, Retweets, favorites, etc.);
- Using or promoting third-party services or apps that claim to get you more followers (such as follower trains, sites promising "more followers fast" or any other site that offers to automatically add followers to your account);

Be sure to read The Twitter Rules (http://bit.ly/FollowingTheRules) to ensure you are compliant and that you are Following the Rules and Best Practices, so your account is never suspended.

HOW TO WIN ON INSTAGRAM

NOTE: This section assumes you have a public Instagram account. If you are new to Instagram, search Google or YouTube using the keywords "how to use Instagram" for online lessons, classes, videos and additional resources.

Although you access Instagram on your computer, and you can like and comment on images, it is a mobile app and you can only upload, and regram, from a mobile device; smartphone or tablet.

If you do not own either device you can get an Instagram account on your computer, but as it's a mobile app you will only be able to like and comment.

If you do enter Instagram contests, be sure to follow me: @TheContestQueen. I post the contest instructions before my entry so you can easily learn by example.

124

Contests on Instagram

Most of the sweepstakes found on Instagram are usually like and comment and sometimes regram or repost. Unlike Facebook and Twitter, most companies do not use Instagram to promote giveaways on other platforms.

Generally, companies that host Instagram contests create them on another platform or page and you submit your entries via Instagram.

Finding Contests on Instagram

As I outlined in the Twitter section of this chapter, finding contests on social media aren't easy. For example, if you type #sweepstakes in the Instagram search field you get over ½ million results. Those are also unfiltered. They are global results and many will not apply to you.

Who to Follow & Why

I find following sponsors and sweeping buddies is the best way to find Instagram giveaways. Following those types of accounts will alert you to new sweepstakes with little effort. Start with sweepers you have met on Facebook and Twitter and go from there.

NOTE: Instagram's feed may be harder for you to scroll through as the images are large-ish. Therefore the more accounts you follow, the harder it may be for you to find contests in between the selfies, OOTD shots (Outfit Of The Day) and food pictures.

Instagram Contests

I ran a social media contest giving away three $25 gift cards. One on Facebook, one on Twitter and one on Instagram.

This is what I posted on Instagram:

I am hosting 3 giveaways!! Win 1 of 3 $25 gift cards on Instagram. (You can win 1 on Facebook & 1 on Twitter.)

1. Follow @TheContestQueen on Instagram.
2. Like this picture.
    Regram this picture tagging @TheContestQueen & #WinWithTheContestQueen
3. One regram entry per person per day.
4. Ends March 4th 2015 at 11:59pm ET.
5. Open only to Canadians.

Check my blog post (link in profile) for further details. This contest is in no way sponsored by Instagram or the company whose gift cards I am giving away.

This is the most difficult platform for me to teach as I am writing this book post on my laptop and the app is on my mobile phone. To make it more confusing, Instagram app is slightly different depending on your smartphone (Android vs iPhone).

If everyone followed the rules, they all would have liked my page, liked the post, regrammed the image using the hashtag #WinWithTheContestQueen and the entry numbers would be equal. They are clearly not. When I selected my potential winner, I checked to see if they followed all the steps. Thankfully they had, so I didn't need to go to the back-ups I had also drawn.

TIP: You must follow all the steps a sponsor posts to be in to win.

Many commented using the hashtag. That is not a regram and wasn't necessary to win, nor was it included as an option when I conducted my drawing.

There are two ways to regram an Instagram image:

1. is to take a screenshot and upload it as a picture.
2. is to use a third-party app.

I prefer to use an app to regram images, versus taking a screen shot. I use Repost on Android and Repost It on Apple iOS. I find it easier for me than taking a screen shot as it also includes all the original poster's text, which is very handy for contesting. I chose to pay the $1.99 for the pro versions because I use the apps daily and I wanted to skip the ads.

This is also my preferred method of contesting while waiting in line or for a meeting, commuting on the train, etc. as it's quick, fun and my odds of winning are better than on Facebook or Twitter (which I do after Instagram if the wait is particularly long).

Regramming

If you take a screenshot of the contest, regramming is only a matter of posting a picture from the Gallery versus taking a picture. You must also remember what account names, tags and hashtags you need to add to the image before finalizing your post.

Each regram app works the same way. When you find an image you want to regram, TAP the THREE DOTS in the upper right hand corner. You will get a pop-up window. SELECT Copy Share URL. CLOSE Instagram. OPEN Repost. The item you selected will appear at the top of the list of items to regram. TAP it. SELECT Repost. SELECT Open Instagram. TAP the RIGHT ARROW in the upper right hand corner. Again, TAP the RIGHT ARROW. In the Write a caption area TAP and HOLD. SELECT PASTE. Here is where you need to Tag People if it is an entry requirement. Then TAP the CHECKMARK in the upper right hand corner.

How Winners are Notified

Similar to Facebook and Twitter, if you are slected as a winner, the contest sponsor will either tag you in a comment on the original post, or in announcement post. They may also send you a Direct Message (DM).

Unlike Facebook and Twitter, where notifications are an automatic part of their platform, you must turn on notifications in Instagram or you could lose out on a big prize.

ဆဩ

Lynn—Whitby, ON

I had to share this story with my local contest club as it was a tough lesson I didn't want any other member to experience.

I started by stating I had good news and bad news. First I broke the bad news.

A local clothing store held a selfie contest. As it was open to both Canada and the United States, I wasn't going to enter it, but I did anyway.

The rules were:

> We're #selfie ready, are you? Stop by any of our locations to enter our #FreshSelfieContest for your chance to win one of four $1,000 shopping sprees. Fresh Selfie Sweepstakes: Chance to win $1000 gift card. NO PURCHASE NECESSARY. Open to US residents (excluding Hawaii & Alaska) and Canadian residents (excluding Québec) who are the age of majority or older in their

respective jurisdictions. Click link in our profile for official rules and how to enter.

What I didn't realize was, the full rules stated all potential winners only had 48 hours to respond to claim their prize.

Within twenty-four (24) hours of the draw, the selected entrants will be notified by a message sent through Instagram® from the Sponsor ("Notification"). Further communications may be made to the selected entrant via an email address provided by the selected entrant upon notification that he/she has been selected as the potential winner. If the selected entrant does not respond within forty-eight (48) hours to the initial message from the Sponsor, the selected entrant will be deemed to have forfeited the Grand Prize.

Even though it was past the deadline, I searched online and called their offices in New York to see if I could still be a winner. Although I pleaded with them, they had to follow their rules. However, they did give me a $100 gift card as a consolation prize.

As I only checked Instagram every few days I didn't get the notification in time and lost out on a big prize. I now have my notifications turned on!

Thankfully I had good news to share with the club. I had won a trip to Italy!! WOOT!! What a fantastic vacation we had that summer.

೫೦೦೮

Here is how you turn on those important notifications.

TAP your PROFILE - the little person on the far right. TAP the THREE TINY DOTS in the upper right (the gear icon in iOS). Scroll down to Push Notifications. The ones you want to select FROM EVERYONE are:

- Comments,
- Instagram Direct Requests,
- Instagram Direct,
- Photos of You,
- Reminders.

When you are notified you will see a tiny Instagram icon in your notification bar at the top of your mobile.

TIP: Make sure you follow the sponsor as it's good contest form, plus most likey they will host another winning opportunity.

How Winners Are Notified on Instagram

If it's a REGRAM contest, the sponsor will either tag you as a winner in another post, or in a comment on the original post. Once again, frequently check your notifications. The notification icon is a little heart on the bottom menu. They may also send you a Direct Message (DM) notifying you about winning.

Sometimes the sponsor asks you to click on the link in their profile to go to the entry page, similar to an online contest, where you fill out a form, you will either get a 'standard' email notification or a phone call.

Loop Giveaways

I am not a fan of Instagram loop giveaways. They can be time consuming and if you are not careful you can wind up in Instagram jail.

Loop giveaways are a valid way for bloggers to garner new followers, but the problem arises when there are too many influencers/bloggers in the loop. The one that turned me off them had forty accounts I had to follow and comment upon. The largest I found had over sixty!

Here is what I believe a good Instagram loop giveaway looks like and what you should avoid. Time wasted could be better spent entering contests elsewhere.

I like Instagram contests as a whole as you enter them from your mobile phone and are perfect for those out-and-about down times; waiting rooms, train commutes, etc.

AS I previously stated most of the giveaways I enter are from the sponsor's post or the sponsor may have partnered with one or two other companies requiring you to follow, but not participate on every account.

Loop giveaways require you to enter on the sponsor's post and then check the image for the tag to take you to the next party in the loop.

Poorly Executed Loop Giveaway
The trap is, a bad Instagram contest looks good on the surface, the rules seem clear, except they do not tell you who is in the loop. It could be five, or it could be fifty, Instagrammers participating.

To me that is crazy. Just entering takes an inordinate amount of time for one prize. The odds of winning ware dismal. I may have wanted to keep following many of the bloggers after the promotion is over, as they usually continue to host giveaways, but will find they are just more loop contests.

NOTE: A real Instagram contest will also have an image, but I do not want to single out any particular blogger so I will only use sample text in my examples.

EXAMPLE TEXT:
Don't be fooled! This is no joke! I've teamed up with a group of amazing ladies to bring you this luxury giveaway! Enter to win an Authentic Louis Vuitton Eva Clutch. You pick the design! (You will receive one Eva clutch shipped directly to you from LV.)

Follow the steps below:
1. Follow me.
2. Like this post.
3. Tap the photo to see where to loop to next! Continue to tap, follow and like until you return back to me. (You must follow everyone involved in this loop. We will check.) You don't want to miss out!

Bonus entries: Tag 3 friends in the comments and/or Repost this photo and tag me.

The Nitty Gritty: Open to to the U.S. And Canada. Entries accepted until 4/4/2015 at 7PM CST. The winner will be announced on 04/03/2015. *Disclaimer: This giveaway is in no way sponsored, endorsed or administered with Instagram or Louis Vuitton. By entering, entrants confirm they are 13+ years of age, release Instagram of responsibility and Agree to Instagram's terms of use.

Also be wary of Instagram giveaways with thin rules or none at all. If you are unsure, before you enter, review an account's profile and feed. It will give you a good idea if the contest is legitimate.

Well Executed Loop Giveaway
A good contest will have: clear and concise rules plus all contest requirements will be right on the image. For example all loop participants are listed.

EXAMPLE TEXT
Celebrate the arrival of Spring and enter to win a $50 PayPal for yourself and ANOTHER $50 for a friend you tag in this Instagram Loop Giveaway.

As you click through the loop to enter to win, you'll meet 4 other fabulous mom bloggers. One random entrant and their fortunate friend will each receive a $50 PayPal cash prize.

TO ENTER:

1. Follow me on Instagram and "like" this photo on Instagram.
2. Tap the photo to see who is next in the loop.
3. Follow her and "like" the giveaway photo on her account.
4. Continue through the loop until you return here.
5. Leave a comment saying you're "done" and tag a friend.

You must follow all 5 hosts and like each loop photo in order to qualify for prizing. The friend you tag can also enter, but she needs to tag a friend other than you. The winner will be chosen randomly after 1 pm EST Saturday April 16th, 2015. The winner and the friend she tagged will be announced in a comment on the giveaway loop post by the contest organizer.

By entering you confirm you are 18+ years of age, release Instagram of responsibility and agree to Instagram's terms of use. This contest is not affiliated with Instagram in any way. Open to US & Canadian residents only (excluding Quebec). Void in whole or in part where prohibited by law.

Instagram Jail

It is possible to find yourself in Instagram Jail. That means you will be blocked from liking and/or commenting.

If you tag 20+ people in various Instagram contests in short succession, you find yourself blocked. It means you have violated Instagram's Comunity Guidelines. http://bit.ly/InstagramCommunityGuidelines

The highlights are:

- Following: you can only follow 7500 accounts/people.
- Likes: you are limited to 350 likes per hour.
- Hashtags: you can only include 30 hashtags per post.
- Characters: you can only use 2200 for both posts and comments.
- Posts: there is no limit to the number of posts.

I have yet to find anything specifically posted on tagging limits. Not even on Instagram.

HOW TO WIN ON PINTEREST

NOTE: This section assumes you have a public Pinterest account. If you are new to Pinterest, search Google or YouTube using the keywords "how to use Pinterest" for online lessons, classes, videos and additional resources.

Unlike Facebook and Twitter that are social media channel that focus on connections and conversations, Pinterest is more akin to Instagram as it's also an image based platform. Where Instagram is a photo sharing channel, Pinterest is a virtual bulletin board.

Remember sticking pictures of things you loved on your bedrooms walls or in your locker? Pinterest is the grown-up virtual version of that. A place where you post pictures of what you like and love. You create boards and you pin pictures to them.

I recommend that each board you create have a theme, which lends itself to easily grouping similar images together. I have contest boards, but I also create an annual vision board and one chock full of recipes I want to try.

Pinterest became a popular social channel with businesses that had visual appeal such as furniture and décor companies, fashion stores and all things food as women make up 85% of the users.

Contests on Pinterest

Contests on Pinterest are known as 'Pin to Win' or 'Pin it to Win it' promotions. Unlike Facebook and Twitter, most companies do not use Pinterest to promote giveaways on other platforms.

Similar to Instagram, companies that host Pinterest contests usually create them on another platform or page and you submit your entries via Pinterest.

Finding Contests on Pinterest

Finding contests on certain social media platforms isn't always easy. For example, if you type #sweepstakes in the Pinterest search field you get a massive unknown quantity of pins. They are also unfiltered. You do get options to futher narrow down your search, but it isn't always practical.

You will also discover that only some of the contests listed are Pin to Win style giveaways. The balance are promotional pins leading you to a sweepstakes on another platform or website.

The best place to find Pin It to Win It contests is on sweepstakes aggregate sites. You will also discover their popularity is far below the number of Facebook, Twitter and Instagram contests you will find.

Pinterest Contests

I did not host a Pin to Win contest to generate an example for this book as I did for the other three popular social platforms, I'll describe what you will need to do to enter this style of sweepstakes.

Some contests ask you to give the board a specific name and even pin specific pictures to it. It is even more important to read the rules for Pinterest contests as most have very detailed guidelines that must be followed for your entry to be eligible. As many are judged, if you do not follow the rules to the letter, you will not win.

To create a board, you must be on your profile page, not on your feed. Then CLICK on the large Add + on the left of the page. You will then get a pop-up window. You must create a board before you can begin pinning to it.

Fill in all the fields as per the contest rules.

TIP: To make it easier to pin, download an app or pin it button; Pinterest Goodies.

When you click on your pin it button on your toolbar or use the pin it icon that pops up when you hover your mouse over an image, you will get the option as to which board you wish to pin the image to. Select the board you created for your contest entry. Each pin gives you an area to add a description. What you put there will depend on the contest rules. Some ask for a specific phrases or hashtags be used. Again, read the rules. (It's why it has always been my #1 entry tip.)

As most Pinterest contests are hosted on another platform, you will usually need to copy the URL of the board you created and paste it onto the entry page.

How Winners are Notified

There are two ways you could be notified of a Pinterest win; within Pinterest itself or via email.

Companies will tag a winner with their handle (i.e. @ContestQueen) or will send you a Direct Message. More likely you will receive an email, or phone call, as most Pin to Win giveaways require you to create a board and then fill out an entry form, like a 'regular' contest.

Similar to Instagram, ensure you turn on notifications. You can find them in the Settings section of your profile. Chose to get notifications from everyone and also receive them by email, just in case you do not login for a few days or have the app on your phone.

Pinterest Jail

Unlink the other social channels I have never been, or know anyone, that has been in Pinterest Jail or had their Pinterest account suspended.

That said, it's possible to get suspended, but it seems much harder than on Facebook, Twitter or Instagram. You can review Pinterest's Acceptable Use Policy to ensure you won't land yourself in jail: http://bit.ly/PinterestUse

NOTE: Google+ currently does not allow sponsors to host giveaways on their platform. Companies can promote contests on Google+ only. Any promotions found there will take you somewhere else to enter. You may wish to have a Google+ account as many sweepstakes give you extra entries if you share on Google+ or if friends enter from your online shares.

*"Remember, the greatest gift is not found in a store
nor under a tree, but in the hearts of true friends."*
Cindy Lew

JOIN A CONTEST CLUB

Sweeping clubs have been around in the United States for decades. The Affadaisies are the most famous sweeping club having been featured in both the book and the movie, The Prize Winner of Defiance, Ohio.

Evelyn Ryan, the story's heroine, and I have something in common. We were both elated to discover the best part of entering contests and sweepstakes is the people you meet, not the wins. I have made contest buddies, sweeping pals and life-long friends from attending club meetings and conventions.

> Of course, my mother was elated to discover other women out in the world who share her love of contesting. Not that she felt alone in her efforts. She had subscribed for years to the two publications no contester would be without: semimonthly Contest Magazine and bi-monthly Contest Worksheet, both of which announced up-coming contests, rules, and deadlines, and offered helpful hints and essays from consistent winners.

> But Dortha was a living breathing contester, and Mom responded to her letter immediately with the name of the winning entry: My Frisk-the-Frigidaire, Clean-the-Cupboards-Bare Sandwich.

> "Well, no wonder I came in second," Dortha wrote in her next letter. "But I'm proud to say I also came in fourth." (This was true. Dortha had won two of the top four prizes in a single contest.) "My fourth place winner was My Gastro-Comical, Tummy-Yummysome Sandwich," Dortha wrote. "And my absolute favorite entry-My Ding-Dong-Double-Decked, Left-the-Kitchen-Wrecked Sandwich-didn't win a thing.

> "By the way, Evelyn, what did you do with the jukebox? Seeburg has offered me $400 or a color TV instead, but $400 doesn't seem like enough money, and I've already won eleven televisions, so I sure don't need another one."

> "Call up Augie Van Brackel," was Mom's advice. "He gave me $500 for my jukebox."

Mom had found a soulmate. In addition to the eleven TVs, Dortha had won thirty-nine radios. And between the two of them, they had seventeen children, hundreds of product labels and box tops (called "qualifiers," or "quallies," in the contest biz), and a single approach to life: "No matter how many kids you have," wrote Dortha, "I'm firmly convinced that a person can find the time to do the things they want to do, and you must want to contest.

"Come to the Affadaisies meeting at my house the first Tuesday of every month," she wrote. "We trade entry blanks, "quallies," and fish stories about the "won" that got away. You'll love it, and besides, I'd love to meet you."

Reprinted with the permission of Simon & Schuster Publishing Group, a Division of Simon & Schuster Inc. from THE PRIZE WINNER OF DEFIANCE, OHIO by Terry Ryan. Copyright © 2001 by Terry Ryan.

The original clubs in 1957 were The Versatillies based in Fort Wayne, IN and The Affadaisies based in Payne, OH. They met once per month in each other's homes, finding it helpful to consult each other improving their entries. In 1980, due to dwindling members they merged both clubs into The Affadaisies. Five of the original The Affadaisies did celebrate their 50th Golden Anniversary and continued to meet on a monthly basis as long as they could. I was lucky enough to attend a meeting and interview them before the original members passed.

L-R: Betty Schmidt, Dortha Schaefer, Alice Bruns, Betty Yearling, Maureen Kennerk and Maria Miller.

Alice Bruns
Alice, a friend of Dortha's, attended one club meeting and was hooked!

Alice's favorite wins were two sets of World Book encyclopedias and four tickets to the Indianapolis 500. She also loved all the little things she won such as: watches, radios, mixers, coffeepots, etc.

Maureen Kennerk

Maureen joined the Affadaisies in 1980. Dortha wrote an article for the Paulding Progress about her hobby of Belly Dancing. They discovered they had a mutual love of contesting.

Maureen began entering on the cusp of the hobby as it made the switch from plentiful contests to mostly sweepstakes. (because of the cost of judging entries for contests as well as being able to attract more entries with the ease of entering a sweepstakes. Maureen prefers contesting to sweepstaking as it challenges her and enters all she can find. Her favorite wins were a trip and a car!

In 1978 Maureen spent three weeks listening day and night to a local radio station to identify 20 history heroes. She then mailed in close to 1000 postcard entries with the correct answers and won a Fiat Spider Convertible in the tiebreaker drawing from all correct entries.

In 1992 in a Stanley Tool contest, Maureen figured out where a virtual treasure was buried at the Winter Olympics from a series of clues that yielded letters to be unscrambled. (At the Giant Slalom Starting Gate was the answer). She wrote her 500 word tiebreaker entry in rhyme describing how she solved the puzzle--which won her a one week trip for four to Hawaii plus a rental car, $500 spending money and $500 in food vouchers.

Maria Miller

Maria is the youngest and newest member of The Affadaisies. She met Dortha in 1987 when she was a freelance writer at the same local newspaper Dortha wrote for. Dortha not only encouraged her to join The Affadaisies, but follow her dream of becoming a writer.

Maria, an avid photographer, puts all her talents to use and also enters photography and essay writing contests. She has enjoyed numerous small wins, mainly cash prizes.

Dortha Schaefer

Betty White won a car for entering a last-line limerick contest and talked Dortha into attending a meeting. The hobby was very addictive for her.

Dortha was so addicted she would even go to the city dump to "quallie hunt." (Get entry qualifiers such as box tops and can labels to be able to submit more entries.)

Her best win was a jukebox. The best part of the win was making lifelong friends with Evelyn Ryan. She also won 11 TVs and 39 radios!

Betty Schmidt
I was not fortunate enough to meet Betty as she had passed away by the time I met The Affidaisies in 2007. Dortha really loved the photo (above) as Betty had been a part of the club since the beginning and wanted to include her and her wonderful memory here.

Betty Yearling
Betty S. invited Betty Y. to her a meeting. At first Betty Y. didn't want to participate but Betty S. "kept on her" until she got hooked on the hobby. She only entered contests, not sweepstakes.

Her funniest win was a pony. Since they lived on a farm they kept him until he began chasing the sheep so they, sadly, sold him.

In 1961 Betty won a trip to Brazil but since she was about to have a baby and couldn't travel she was able to convince the sponsor to sell the trip for her.

If you are lucky enough to own a copy of the 1964 Pillsbury Bake-Off Cookbook, make her winning Party Pork Barbecue recipe.

Make sure you don't miss out on all the fun and join or start a club today!

STORY: Teresa shows us the benefits of being a sweepstakes club member and how entering as a team, everybody wins.

ଔଓଷ

Teresa—Rochester NY
Our local television station has an annual backyard BBQ party contest. Winners are drawn weekly. Each winner gets a BBQ party hosted by the local TV weatherman along with food and drink for 25 people. The station also does a remote broadcast from the winner's backyard.

As a club, we all enter faithfully every year. Three years in a row one member has been lucky enough to win, giving our club a free summer party.

All the weekly winners get invited back to the station at the end of the summer and put into a grand prize drawing for a hot tub. Our club has never won the grand prize, but I am sure one year one of us will!

ଔଓଷ

Sweeping and Contest Clubs

Sweeping and contest clubs meet, on average, once per month at a local restaurant or a member's home. Contact your local club to get specific meeting details.

The clubs listed are the ones that have agreed to be in this book. There are many more sweeping clubs in the U.S. and Canada. If you do not see one listed for your area/region, you may find clubs by searching the Internet, within sweepstakes specific websites or attending a convention to meet fellow sweepers from your region.

United States

ALABAMA

Pensacola Panhandlers
From Crestview FL to Gulf Shores AL
Contact Paula at paulapets@att.net or 850-292-8214

ARIZONA

Saguaro Sweepers
Phoenix, AZ
Contact Paula at fivefrys@cox.net

The Southern UT Sweepstakes Club
St. George, Washington, Ivins, Hurricane, Cedar City & LaVerkin UT, Beaver AZ, Mesquite NV & surrounding areas.
Contact Paula at Bubbaadams5@aol.com or 435.986.4156

CALIFORNIA

The Central (Fresno) CA Sweepers
Fresno, CA
Contact Arlene at am3851956@yahoo.com or 559.431.1316

Inland Empire Sweepers
Fontana, CA
Contact Denise at denise@iesweepers.com or www.iesweepers.com

San Diego Sweepers
San Diego, CA
Contact Mary at maryk02@san.rr.com or 858.672.3470 or Steve at sdadolf@san.rr.com or 858.451.2130

DISTRICT OF COLUMBIA
Chesapeake Crabs Sweepstakers
Baltimore, Frederick, MD & surrounding areas
Contact Brenda at MDCrab3@aol.com or 301.371.6161

The Metro Sweepers
Washington, DC & MD & VA metropolitan areas
Contact Linda-Jo at holalj@verizon.net or Becky at rescario@gmail.com

FLORIDA
Central Florida Sweepstakers
Orlando, FL & surrounding area
Contact Diana at dflory076@aol.com or Cecilia at cebbird@yahoo.com

Mid-Florida Sunshine Sweepers
Marion, Citrus, Levy & Hernando counties, FL
Contact John at bam0607@embarqmail.com or 352.347.6064

Pensacola Panhandlers
From Crestview FL to Gulf Shores AL
Contact Paula at paulapets@att.net or 850-292-8214

SW Florida Gulf Sweepers
Vanice FL & Manatee, Sarasota and Charlotte counties
Contact BJ at bj.grant@att.net

Tampa Bay Sweepaneers
Tampa Bay, FL
Contact Nancy at 5kleins@verizon.net

ILLINOIS
Northern Illinois Dream Sweepers
Rockford IL
Contact Sheryl at holdensheryl@hotmail.com

The Prize Magnets
Aurora IL
Contact us at mhislop52@yahoo.com

The Quad City Winners
Western IL & Eastern IA
Contact Sue at bowlinsuzy@yahoo.com or 563.785.4982

INDIANA
The Hoosier Winners
Plymouth, IN
Contact Deb at djhouin@msn.com

IOWA
Central Iowa Winners
DeMoines, IA
Contact Laura at laurak.ostrem@gmail.com

The Quad City Winners
Western IL & Eastern IA
Contact Sue at bowlinsuzy@yahoo.com or 563.785.4982

KENTUCKY
Kentucky Lucky Sweepers
Florence KY
Contact Terry at sweepertjs@yahoo.com

MARYLAND
Chesapeake Crabs Sweepstakers
Baltimore, Frederick, MD & surrounding areas
Contact Brenda at MDCrab3@aol.com or 301.371.6161

The Metro Sweepers
Washington, DC & MD & VA metropolitan areas
Contact Linda-Jo at holalj@verizon.net or Becky at rescario@gmail.com

MICHIGAN
Michigan Wolverine Winners
Royal Oak, MI
Contact Al at michigansweepers2002@yahoo.com or 586.791.7819

MT Town Sweepers
Mount Pleasant, MI
Contact Tena at bill48877@hotmail.com

MINNESOTA
Clean Sweepers
Bloomington MN
Contact Mary at marywhitescarver@gmail.com

MISSISSIPPI
Hub City Sweeping Club
Southern MS
Contact Julian at juliansaintthomas@gmail.com

NEVADA
Las Vegas Sweepstakes Enthusiasts
Las Vegas, NV
Contact Pam at pmooney277@aol.com or 720.879.1679

The Southern UT Sweepstakes Club
St. George, Washington, Ivins, Hurricane, Cedar City & LaVerkin UT,
Beaver AZ, Mesquite NV & surrounding areas.
Contact Paula at Bubbaadams5@aol.com or 435.986.4156

NEW JERSEY
South Jersey Sweepers
Mays Landing, NJ
Contact Marge at kittystamp@comcast.net or 609.909.1518

NEW MEXICO
Red Hot Chilie's
Albuquerque NM
Contact Wendy at 27pisces@msn.com

NEW YORK
The Big Apple Sweepstakers
New York City, NY & surrounding metropolitan areas
Contact Steve at animanni1@aol.com

The Lucky Lilacs
Rochester, NY
Contact Terry at tmyoung@rochester.rr.com

A Real Bunch of Winners
Upstate NY, Albany NY & Area
Contact Joy at mjoymayo@aol.com or 518-731-8076

NORTH CAROLINA
Carolina Sweepers
Charlotte, Concord & Kannapolis, NC
Contact Sharon at sharonwin1@aol.com or 704.549.1674

Virginia Beach Prize Patrol
Virginia Beach, VA & NC area
Contact Ret at ret2win@aol.com

OHIO
Lucky Bucks
Columbus, OH
Contact Diane at slags68@aol.com

Northern Ohio Sweeps Club
Cleveland/Akron and suburbs
Contact Rita at Sams842@yahoo.com or Patty at pat.kettren@yahoo.com

OREGON
The Oregon Lucky Ducks Sweepstakes Club
Salem, OR
Contact Mike and Julie at marchison@aol.com or Vickie at
valsetzvic@gmail.com or 503.930.7695

SOUTH CAROLINA
South Carolina Midland Sweepers
Columbia, SC
Contact Barbara at budlake09@yahoo.com or 864.423.2054

The Winning Team Sweeps Club
Clemson, SC
Contact Ingrid at ingridjjan@bellsouth.net or 864.646.7391

TENNESSEE
UcanWin2
Knoxville, TN
Contact Judy at jmcne45379@yahoo.com

TEXAS
Austin Sweepers
Austin, TX
Contact Gail at dgtwight@sbcglobal.net

UTAH
UT UPS Chasers
Taylorsville, UT
Contact Diane at sandybeaches58@gmail.com

The Southern UT Sweepstakes Club
St. George, Washington, Ivins, Hurricane, Cedar City & LaVerkin UT,
Beaver AZ, Mesquite NV & surrounding areas.
Contact Paula at Bubbaadams5@aol.com or 435.986.4156

VIRGINIA
Chesapeake Crabs Sweepstakers
Baltimore, Frederick, MD & surrounding areas
Contact Brenda at MDCrab3@aol.com or 301.371.6161

The Metro Sweepers
Washington, DC & MD & VA metropolitan areas
Contact Linda-Jo at holalj@verizon.net or Becky at rescario@gmail.com

NOVASWEEPERS
Northern VA & surrounding areas
Contact Velma at dexrock@aol.com

The Old Dominion Sweepers
Richmond VA
Contact Linda at LindaMartin737@comcast.net

Virginia Beach Prize Patrol
Virginia Beach, VA & NC area
Contact Ret at ret2win@aol.com

WISCONSIN
The Fortunate Cookies
Madison, WI
Contact Joyce at tommyjoy66@aol.com

Canada

BRITISH COLUMBIA
Lower Mainland Contest Club
Vancouver, BC
Contact Harmony at hpoisson@gmail.com

ONTARIO
T.O. Wanna Winners
Toronto, ON
Contact: t.o.wanna@hotmail.com
Blog: towannawinners.blogspot.com

The Winner's Circle
Whitby ON and surrounding areas
Contact Carolyn at clubs@contestqueen.com

You can even start your own club. For more information, email
sweepingclubs@contestqueen.com

*STORY: Not only can being part of a club bring fellowship into your hobby
and life, it can also bring new adventures, memories and wins.*

ഇന്ദ

Tracy—Burke, VA

Fabio is the Nova Sweeper's sweepstakes idol. We have an 8 x 10
autographed copy of him framed and we draw for it every month at our
meetings. It was originally won by one of our members in an online instant
win game. Whoever wins the photo for the month takes it home and is
guaranteed "Good Luck" for that month. Fabio has brought great prizes, trips

144

and cash just to name a few. Fabio is sometimes known as "FABIA" when the men in the group win it. It has been adorned with coconuts, grass skirts, candied hearts and four leaf clovers. It has been a great source of luck, fun and laughs!

Fabio has been to several conventions. It was first taken to the Northeast Mini Sweepstakes Convention at Hershey, PA in 2006. It brought the member who won him that month lots of nice wins. It has also attended 18th Annual National Sweepstakes Convention in Dearborn, MI. There it brought the monthly winner over $500.00 in gift cards, a Motown CD and some nice sweepstakes supplies.

The Power of Fabio is gaining Nova Sweepers recognition amongst fellow sweepers. We are happy to share the luck with anyone who wants to touch our Fabio photo. Of course, you have to believe in order to receive. We are believers.

&)(&

Conventions

The first Annual National Sweepstakes Convention (ANSC) was held in Michigan in 1989. It is run each year on a volunteer basis by a different sweeping club, so the convention moves from city-to-city and state-to-state.

There are heaps of activities at each convention, including featured speakers, raffles, vendors, breakout sessions, road trips, sightseeing, etc. Since each convention is in a new and different location, no two conventions are exactly alike which makes attending every year an adventure.

Further enhancing the experience is the opportunity to meet online sweeping buddies. Putting faces to names, trading winning stories along with tips and tricks are all a part of the convention you cannot put a price on.

What also cannot be explained, but must be experienced, is the exhilarating energy of hundreds sweepstakers in one room. Especially, when they have a bag full of freebies and are winning prizes. There is less screaming at a rock concert!

There are also regional events, meetings, banquets and mini-conventions.

NOTE: For up-to-date convention information, please visit the Resources section of www.contestqueen.com.

Meet Online

Another way to meet fellow sweepers is to join an online group. Being a member of various online communities has also led me to several face-to-face meetings and making real friends. I feel posting sweepstakes and answers has helped me win because it follows the adage you reap what you sow. (See chapter, Attracting Luck.)

Sweepers may also post when they will be visiting another city on vacation or a business trip. Fellow sweepers will then meet them for a drink at the airport (on a stopover), for lunch, or take them on a tour of their city. I have had the pleasure of meeting many fellow sweepers this way.

You may notice that people participating in the group seem to follow the 80/20 rule. i.e. 80% of the sweepstakes are posted by 20% of the members. Some of the reasons the majority of people do not post sweepstakes are: 1) some members are just better at finding sweepstakes, 2) sometimes someone will go to post a sweepstakes or answer and find that it has already been posted and 3) some members have more time to post sweepstakes and answers.

Not all members will participate in the group. I call those people "lurkers." They enjoy the hobby of sweeping and they learn about all the new sweepstakes and contests from the active members of the group, but they do not give back by posting anything they find or post their winnings. It is impossible to know what percentage of a group are lurkers because you will never hear from them. Don't be a lurker. The enjoyment I get from this hobby is just not the thrill of winning but the joy I get from my sweeping friends. I feel you will miss out on a fantastic part of this hobby if you lurk. (See sections, Newsletters or Websites, for a list of sweepstaking websites that also host an online group or forum and Facebook for groups.)

> *"Play fair. Don't hit people.*
> *Say you're sorry when you hurt somebody."*
> Robert Fulghum

Online Sweepstaking Etiquette

This section could also be called common courtesy. It is "Do unto others as you would have others do unto you." Since this book's focus is primarily on Internet sweeping, the etiquette will focus primarily on how to behave within an online community or forum.

Post complete messages. Before clicking the Send button, review your message to ensure all relevant sweepstakes information is included. You should type a meaningful subject and then include a direct link to the sweepstakes and possibly the rules, what the prize is, eligibility, how many times one can enter and the end date of the sweepstakes.

EXAMPLE:
New Sweep @ Contest Queen
http://www.contestqueen.com
win a car—open to the U.S.—one entry per person per day—ends Dec 31st
GOOD LUCK,
Carolyn
in Oshawa

TIP: Always include the full URL including the http:// to make the link clickable in the message.

If you post a message and it doesn't appear immediately, please **be patient**. The Internet is not always instant. I have seen the same message posted three and four times because someone didn't give the server a chance to process the original message.

DO NOT TYPE YOUR MESSAGE ALL IN CAPITALS. Not only is it hard to read, it is usually interpreted as shouting. If you can't use the shift key easily, all lowercase is much easier on the eyes and less likely to be misinterpreted.

Most forums will not allow you to send attachments. This is to prevent viruses, pornography, and other unpleasantness from proliferating to group members, and as a courtesy to members who have slow Internet connections.

Do not forward other's postings or messages outside the group without getting permission from the author first. It is rude and inconsiderate, and posting a sweepstakes you didn't originally find to another group is disrespectful to both the group and the poster.

As a follow up to this, if you do need to forward information to a group (or to individuals, for that matter), **delete any email addresses from the original message before you send**. This is important--you wouldn't give out an acquaintance's phone number or home address without their permission, so don't give out their email address either. Plus you put them in danger to be hacked, be sent viruses, or worse.

NOTE: I post sweepstakes to many groups. However, I only post sweepstakes that I find myself. If another group member found it, I do not cross-post.

147

Post a Thank You on the original post, when you win something big. People like to be appreciated and to see their efforts of finding sweepstakes are indeed helping others win. It does make a difference.

Before you reply to a posting, **think about whether or not the entire group needs to see your reply**. If your posting is of a personal nature or directed to one person, email them directly.

Read everyone else's posts before replying to one. A subject quickly becomes a "dead horse" when people do not do this.

If you are posting a message that is not about sweeping or off topic, please **make sure you post it in the appropriate forum.**

When entering a sweepstakes that asks for referrals, **do not refer anyone without their permission first**.

TIP: For more Internet etiquette and tips you can go to: http://bit.ly/InternetEtiquette or search the Internet using the word "netiquette".

"A snake lurks in the grass."
Virgil

PLAY SAFE

One of the biggest concerns or reservations people tell me they have about entering contests and sweepstakes on the Internet is the possible dangers. They always ask if I get a lot of spam or viruses from entering online. I do not.

The sad reality of being connected to the Internet is you must protect your computer or mobile device, regardless if you are entering sweepstakes or not. There are many nasty computer viruses, spyware, malware, etc. that could infect your device, therefore you need to protect yourself.

When you are online you simply need to be aware of these hazards and ensure that you have the proper tools running on your machine to keep the threats out.

The information on this topic is vast, large and very technical. There is an entire industry whose only purpose is to protect us against the "bad guys". Not unlike a city that has a police force or a country that has military.

Be aware, while much of what you are about to read may sound scary, do not let it prevent you from using the Internet for sweeping. Yes, there are dangers but they can be managed. Driving in your car can be dangerous, but you don't lock yourself in your house because of that, do you?

These are the most common problems you may encounter and the most popular solutions to correct them.

NOTE: If you have any computer security issues not listed below, use Google to source out a specific solution.

SPAM

Spam is a common term for bulk, unsolicited emails, which are often inappropriate or irrelevant. Computer users can get spam from many different sources: memberships, subscriptions, surveys, friends or colleagues with viruses or Trojans, and the list goes on. For the most part, spam is an annoyance. If you recognize the sender and they provide an Unsubscribe option, then use it. Often, spammers use software, called bots, harvesters or spiders, to search websites for email addresses. If you *don't* remember the

149

sender, don't bother to use the unsubscribe procedure; you don't want to confirm they've reached a valid email.

Malware

Malware is short for MALicious softWARE, and is any software used to disrupt the operation of a computer, gather confidential information, or to gain access via a back door to computer systems or networks in order to disrupt or gather information. When installed on a computer, malware makes unauthorized changes to the system and settings, collect and transmit data, corrupt or encrypt files and bury the user under various forms of unwanted advertising.

Malware can take the form of viruses, Trojans, root kits, spyware, adware, or ransom ware.

Viruses

Viruses are a form of malware, or programs/bits of malicious code, which is downloaded and installed on your computer surreptitiously and without your consent. They can be acquired via infected email or from infected websites, and can copy and install themselves over and over. They are also capable of replicating and sending themselves out to a user's entire contact list, as well as addresses in both sent and received messages. Viruses can be as harmless as changing your default web browser, or they can cause serious damage by corrupting your operating systems, installed programs or data.

One of the first ways to protect yourself from infection is to install virus and malware protection software which updates its definitions regularly. In addition, an additional, common sense means, is to not open emails from unfamiliar senders, not to click on any links in unfamiliar emails and to not download files or programs from sketchy websites or file sharing software (bit torrent etc.).

Spyware

Spyware is software that is installed on the computer of an individual or organization without the user's knowledge and/or consent. Spyware is used to covertly gather information on the host computer and relay that information to a third party, or to exert some sort of control over the system. This is sometimes benign, sometimes malicious. What is gathered can be something as insignificant as internet surfing activities such as shopping, news, reading, entertainment and sent to advertisers without the inclusion of personal information. It can also be used to gather this personal information like banking information, tax returns, and other sensitive data and sold to criminals.

Adware

Adware is a term for any sort of software that goes beyond the normal advertising experienced when using freeware or shareware. These programs too are installed without the user's consent, or even without their knowledge. Sometimes the programs even generate advertising when they aren't even running.

Internet cookies can be considered a form of spyware or adware since websites install them on systems and there won't be anything to inform the user of this activity. However, these cookies can provide even more information to malicious spyware and adware.

Installation of adware can result in "browser hijacking" that redirects the users browsing to websites with questionable content, bombards the user with "popups" and "popunders", and often the "uncloseable window" which opens more than one new popup or popunder each time a browser window is closed.

Adware can even be installed along with a legitimate program as a type of "bonus", such as browser add-ons, so be cautious and read all end user agreements and data disclosure statements carefully. If you accept, then you have given consent and it is no longer considered spying.

Ransomware

Ransomware is seeing a resurgence in the malware game, after a brief appearance in the late 1980's, the most prominent being one called CryptoLocker. Like all other forms of malware, it is installed without the consent of the user, or by falsely obtaining consent claiming to be something other than what it really is, or claiming to do something it doesn't.

Typically, ransomware is installed through a virus or Trojan. The user clicks on a link in an email and the software is installed, the link takes the user to an infected website, or the user unknowingly visits an infected website.

The user gets a message in a dialog box on their screen clato be from some government agency, such as the FBI or the user's "local police department" with a claim that their computer has been scanned and found to contain illegal content such as pornography, pirated software or media. The user is told their system has been restricted or their data files have been encrypted and access will not be restored until payment (ransom) has been made. This can be amounts from a few hundred to tens of thousands of dollars.

151

Use of virus or malware protection software can prevent the installation of ransomware, however installation of the Trojan is often not detected until the encryption process is either underway or completed. Take caution when opening emails from names you don't recognize, or visiting new unknown websites, and don't click on odd dialog boxes or links!

Protecting Your Computer

Since the first virus was released to the wild, there has been software created to protect computers from various forms of malware, available as individual programs and as suites of software. They are available as paid programs and for home use are often free.

Most programs will passively and actively scan the computer, which means you can run the program and have a scan run on request, and it will also run in the background while other programs are being used and scan for malware while you do something completely unrelated. Files used by the system and user will be scanned, and so will websites the user visits and emails that are read. This means that even if a system check is not started by the user, if anything shows up that contains code that is malicious, or behaves like malware, the protection software will notify the user. These systems can also be programmed to scan the computer on a regular schedule, such as nightly or weekly.

All protection programs *should* have both active and passive scanning capabilities for complete protection. Also make certain your protection software has its malware definitions updated regularly as new threats appear as often as dozens to hundreds per week.

Top Protection Packages

The computer and mobile applications listed below were the highest rated at the time of this publication. In the past, most programs protected your computer against one threat. Now developers offer full service protection packages improving your overall computer or mobile security while at the same time reducing the cost (as you do no longer have to buy every element individually). Many even have free trial offers allowing you to test the program before you buy.

Avast
www.avast.com

AVG
www.avg.com

Bitdefender
www.bitdefender.com

Emsisoft
www.emsisoft.com

ESET
www.eset.com

F-Secure
www.f-secure.com

G Data AntiVirus
www.gdata-software.com

Kaspersky
www.kaspersky.ca

Malwarebytes
www.malwarebytes.com

McAfee
http://bit.ly/McAfeeSecurity

Norton
http://ca.norton.com/

Panda Security
www.pandasecurity.com

Spybot
www.safer-networking.org

Trend Micro
www.trendmicro.ca

Webroot
www.webroot.com

"I've found that luck is quite predictable.
If you want more luck, take more chances.
Be more active. Show up more often. "
Brian Tracy

YOU'RE A WINNER!

Typically, you will be notified of a win by one of the following ways: by telephone, email, courier, or mail, along with range of social media platforms based upon your original method of entry. Most of my sweepstakes win notifications have been by phone. I get notified via telephone and email almost evenly, and I have only had a handful of couriered notifications. **(Sometimes, prizes just arrive in the mail. I love those!)**

NOTE: Experiential prizing is the number one thing most people want to win and the adventure is something they remember their whole lives. Marketers take note!!

The Call

The person calling will ask for the potential winner, introduce themselves and their company, usually mention the sweepstakes name (e.g. Escape to Paradise Sweepstakes) and depending on the value of the prize along with what was required on the entry form.

Write down all pertinent information regarding the caller: get the caller's name, company name and phone number. This is important, because if you need to contact the judging agency, sweepstakes management company or the sponsor regarding the sweepstakes, rules, affidavit and release forms or the prize, you need to know where to begin.

TIP: Keep a small note pad, pen and calculator by every phone in the house (even with your cell phone) in case you are called. I have interviewed many people who lost out on prizes because they were not prepared!

One time, I was driving in my car and I took a winning notification call on my cell phone. Obviously, I was not able to write down the name and number of the person I spoke with. Murphy's Law was hard at work on that win. I keep a spreadsheet of all my wins (see sample following) and I know when a prize has taken longer than the standard 4-8 weeks (usually after the end-date of the promotion) to arrive. The only thing I knew was who the sweepstakes sponsor was, so I began there. It took me two weeks to finally speak to the sweepstakes management company. It took a total of sixteen weeks for my prize to arrive. What I do now is let the person know I am driving and I ask them to call me back at an appropriate time.

CONTEST WINS 2014							
Date	Prize	Where	Value	Received	Entry	Type	Sub-type
Jan 24	Prevage Prize Pack	Dave Lackie	$634.00	x	online	retweet	
Jan 29	2 Movie Passes - The Lego Movie	Get Tickets	$25.00	x	online	1x	
	JANUARY TOTAL		$659.00				
Feb 3	Book - Kiss My Glass	Good Reads	$8.73	x	online	1x	
Feb 4	Book - Goldenland Past Dark	Good Reads	$18.95	x	online	1x	
Feb 6	Book - Find Momo	Good Reads	$14.95	x	online	1x	
Feb 12	Book - The Weird That Strings the Hangman's Bag	Good Reads	$18.95	x	online	1x	
Feb 13	Blender	Europe's Best	$26.00	x	online	game	1x per hour
Feb 14	$100 Target Gift Card	Pickering Town Centre	$100.00	x	online	Instagram	
Feb 16	Books - Savage Harvest & Tragic Quest for Primitive Art	Good Reads	$26.99	x	online	1x	
Feb 17	Book - Fire in the Unnameable Country	Good Reads	$30.00	x	online	1x	
Feb 20	Book - Breakpoint Nereis	Good Reads	$18.95	x	online	1x	
Feb 20	2 Tickets - St. Party's Day Party	Get Connected E-Solutions	$60.00	x	online	Facebook	
Feb 21	Book - Making it Sustainable Culture in a Digital Age	Good Reads	$24.95	x	online	1x	
Feb 22	Coupon for Lindt Chocolate	Lindt	$2.00	x	online	instant win	
Feb 23	Book - Adverse Possession	Good Reads	$8.95	x	online	1x	
Feb 25	2 Ticket - Distillery District Walking Tour w/Segway Ontario	Attractions Ontario	$38.00	x	online	1x	
	FEBRUARY TOTAL		$393.42				
Mar 2	Forrest Gump Prize Pack	Random House	$45.99	x	online	Twitter	party
Mar 3	Book - Forever's Promise	Good Reads	$7.27	x	online	1x	
Mar 8	DVD - Icy Soldiers	Mr. Will Wong	$25.00	x	online	Twitter	Facebook
Mar 10	Book - Paranormal Keepers	Good Reads	$17.78	x	online	1x	
Mar 10	Makeup Brushes	Revlon	$15.99	x	online	Facebook	like & share
Mar 11	Prize Pack - Hudson's Bay Hat, Mitts & Scarf	7 Eleven	$35.00	x	phone	text	daily
Mar 13	2 Tickets - Cabaret, Shaw Festival	Wonderlist	$150.00	x	online	1x	Wootox
Mar 15	6-pack Carlsberg	Carlsberg	$12.00	x	in-person	Twitter	
Mar 25	Book - The Chance	Good Reads	$8.99	x	online	1x	
Mar 27	A Pair of Shoes	Tiger of Sweden	$239.00	x	in-person	Twitter	Instagram
	MARCH TOTAL		$556.96				

NOTE: If you would like to download a blank copy of the spreadsheet to track your wins, check the Resources section of my website under Contestors, Step 1, Online Contests.

TIP: If you are not ready to speak to the judging agency or company because you are driving, your kids are screaming, you're too nervous and want to calm down, or any other reason, ask them to call you back and give them an appropriate time (don't just say "call me back later," though, because it sounds like you're trying to avoid them—give them a specific range of times). If possible, get their name and number.

If you are entering others that live in the same household and they are not available at the time "the call" comes in, take a message for the potential winner, again ensuring you write down all the pertinent information. If no one is home, a voicemail message is usually left. However, I have seen official rules state that if they cannot reach a potential winner, they will not leave a message and another name will be drawn.

Depending on the sweepstakes rules, you will either be sent your prize directly or you may have to fill-out, sign and send back an affidavit or release forms before you are able to claim your prize.

The Letter

Letters arrive either via USPS or Canada Post in your regular mail, by registered mail, or via a courier such as FedEx, Purolator, or UPS. The notification usually includes a congratulatory letter along with the affidavits and release forms. You are generally given a few methods to send back the forms: mail, fax, email (after you scan the forms) or by courier.

TIP: I get my mail in a community mailbox in my complex (aka super mailbox), and don't check the one in beside the front door very often. One day I discovered a Purolator flexible plastic envelope stuffed in there. I have no idea how long it had been there.

STORY: Vicki discovered you should check every possible drop off area around your home for winning notifications.

೪つ೧೩

Vickie—Dallas, OR

If you have home delivery of dairy products be sure and check your delivery box for prizes. Ours is right by our front door and our delivery guy comes Monday morning, so I leave my order slip out Sunday night. One Sunday at 11:30pm I lifted the lid to put my order slip in and noticed a FedEx envelope. I opened the envelope and was notified I had just won $50,000 in a Sony sweepstakes! FedEx had left the envelope sometime between the prior Monday and Saturday. Eeek! I had no idea it was in there. Better than Easter! Woo Hoo!!

೪つ೧೩

The Email

Most of my winning notifications come via email. Many people are wary of opening emails stating they have won something due to past experience with fraudulent correspondence. (See chapter, Avoiding Scams) A legitimate email will be similar to a phone call. It will contain the sweepstakes name, possibly what you have won, the company name (of either the sponsor or the judging agency) and who to contact. You will usually be asked to respond/reply to the email within a specified period of time to claim your prize. Most people do remember what promotions they have entered, recognize the sweepstakes name and will know if it is a legitimate email. If you are unsure, call the contact at the bottom of the email.

TIP: If you are not scanning and emailing back the affidavit, ensure you keep a copy in case the originals are lost in the mail. If you send the forms back by certified mail you have additional proof you sent them back.

My recommendation for any contester who uses Gmail, or any other email system, with filtering is to set up a whitelist filter that doesn't flag as Spam anything that might contain a winning notification.

157

Yes, it results in actual spam sitting in my inbox, but for me it has caught winning emails that otherwise would go to Spam. I still do review my Spam folder daily, as am paranoid I might not notice something important.

My "winning contest email" whitelist filter includes:

1. Anything with a file attachment.

2. Anything that includes the words:

"congratulations" OR
"release form" OR
"grand prize" OR
"first prize" OR
"1st prize" OR
"daily prize" OR
"redeem" OR
"skill testing" OR
"respond by" OR
"another winner" OR
"for entering" OR
"your entry" OR
"witness" OR
"declaration" OR
"fulfillment"

3. Actions for the filter are:

- Star it.
- Apply Label: Contesting or Sweeping.
- Never send it to Spam.
- Always mark it as important.

Reprinted by permission of Ethan Hall-Beyer.

STORY: I never count my wins until the month is officially over. Tina sent this great story of why "it ain't over 'til it's over".

୨୦୧୪

Tina—Wapakoneta, OH

It was December 31st, 2003 at about 2:00pm. Wins were good that year. I had won a digital camera, an Alaskan cruise for my daughter, $500 GC for my son, a computer monitor, $200 worth of Craftsman tools for my husband, Joe, a watch, a washer, $250 worth of CDs, a trip to the CMA Awards, about $300 in groceries and a multitude of other small nice prizes. I certainly had nothing to complain about. Still, most of those larger wins had come earlier in the year and I had been having "vibes"... the ones you get when you feel a good win coming on. I said to Joe, "Gee, I thought I would have one more really good win this year." "Well", Joe said, "I saw the mailman go by. I'll go check for you." "Nope, nothing exciting." Ever the unsinkable optimist, I said "But there's still time for UPS or FedEx! It ain't over 'til it's over!" Joe looked at me sympathetically. He was no longer a Doubting Thomas. He knew all too well the thrill of winning, but the year was almost over.

At exactly 4:00pm I glanced out the window just in time to see the FedEx truck come backing up our driveway. My daughter, who was home for the holidays heard our excitement and bounded down the stairs. "Mom, I should have told you. I ordered some CDs from Amazon and had it sent here." Yeah, we all agreed. That was probably it. Then I watched as the driver emerged from the "Lucky Trucky," as it is referred to around our house, with nothing but an envelope in his hand. That was not Amy's order from Amazon! It was unleashed excitement after that!

That envelope held the news that I was a 2nd prize winner in the Lysol $50,000 Scholarship Sweepstakes! I had won $5,000 on New Year's Eve!

Now, when my wins come a little slower, that memory picks me up. You never know when that big win is 'just around the corner'. I remember that snowy New Year's Eve and remind myself that 'it ain't over 'til it's over!'

‽☙

The Text, Tag, Etc.

As technology advances, so do the number of ways a company can reach out to you to either announce you are a potential or official winner. Depending on the original entry method you may also be notified via text, a tag on Facebook, a mention on Twitter or Instagram, etc.

TIP: Set up a Google Alert for your name and you will be notified by email if your name is used online. As Google improves its social media searching, the alerts also improve. https://www.google.com/alerts

Prizes, Prizes, Everywhere!

Have you ever won something and thought, "Why did I enter this sweepstakes? I didn't want to win this. What was I thinking? Now what am I going to do with it?"

There are several things you can do with prizes you don't want:

1. You could *share* your win. If you can't use a prize give it to someone you know who would really like, enjoy and appreciate it. (See chapter, Attracting Luck.)

2. You could *sell* your win. eBay, Craigslist or Kijiji are popular websites for selling anything and everything.

3. You could *trade* your win. You could offer the trade at a sweepstakes club meeting or post a message on an online group or Facebook.

4. You could *gift* your win. I know many people save their winnings for the holiday season and give them away as gifts to ease the financial strain on their pocket books.

5. You could *donate* your win. Another option is to donate you prize(s) to various charities. Many companies and organizations ask for new unwrapped items for children of all ages and their families. (See chapter, Attracting Luck.)

STORY: Evelyn won a secondary prize she deemed to be "worthless." One man's trash is another man's treasure.

ഇരു

Evelyn—Queen Anne, MD

It all started with my entering a one entry per person sweepstakes called "It's A Very Shady *Xmas*" in 2004.

Around February of the next year a package arrived unannounced. Inside were these bright blue, and I mean bright blue, sized 10 men's Custom Air Slim Shady (Eminem) Nike tennis shoes and an autographed card. I don't have any one in the family who would be in need of those shoes so I put them away and forgot all about them.

It was nearing the next Christmas and my daughter was out of work so I gave them to her to sell on eBay thinking she would maybe get a $100 if she was lucky. Well, the auction went up and she kept getting many emails from people to buy them direct. She declined all of the offers so as not to get in trouble with eBay for selling on the side. We watched the shoes slowly click up in price day after day. Finally, the auction time was near and bids had reached $1,800 we were in total shock! This was truly going to be a good Christmas for my daughter as the bills would be paid and there would be extra for presents.

The last few minutes of the auction were very exciting. The counter was climbing on the number of views of the webpage by about 25 every time we could hit the refresh button. Who would have ever thought? Well, when all was said and done, the auction ended at $3,500!! Can you believe those bright blue shoes went from a win to a windfall?!

৪০৫৪

"Winning is important to me, but what brings me real joy is the experience of being fully engaged in whatever I'm doing."
Phil Jackson

YOU WIN SOME, YOU LOSE SOME

I wanted to include a different type of story in this book. A story of great excitement, anticipation, disappointment and finally hope.

I received an email stating I was a Grand Prize Contestant in the Coca-Cola® Mac's Win-a-Mini Sweepstakes. At first I thought I won a Mini. I called Craig up from his office to read the email to determine what I had really won while I stopped hyperventilating. What "Grand Prize Contestant" meant was, I was one of a hundred chosen for the opportunity to go to Paramount Canada's Wonderland (an amusement park north of Toronto) on the following Saturday and participate in a key-turn drawing for a chance to win a Mini Cooper Classic. 1 in 100 odds of winning a car was really good!

I use all the techniques I talk about in the Attracting Luck chapter. Now, all I seemed to do 24/7 was meditate, think or dream about winning the Mini. I went down to the local Mini dealership, studied the key, took a test drive and bought a Mini t-shirt to wear at the draw. I even had my insurance company give me a quote.

The rules stated I was to arrive at the park three hours before the draw. Since Craig and Nicole came with me, we had time to wander the park, look at all the cool sights and have a bite to eat.

At the appointed time, we gathered at the showcase where the draw was being held. The Mini Cooper Classic was up on the stage surrounded by balloons and lit up with spot lights. (New cars can really shine!) The sweepstakes management company representative came out and gave us a brief overview of what was going to take place. There were sixty keys, each in a little box, on the display table. Wait…Only sixty?! It turns out that sixty out of the hundred potential car winners replied with the proper forms and actually showed up for the draw. My odds had just gotten much better!

They would draw a name from the drawing drum, that person would come up, select a box from the table, go to the car, get in the car and see if their

161

key started the engine. If the key started the engine that person would win the car. Potentially, the drawing could end right away if the first person selected the winning key.

They drew the first name. Not me. The fellow went up, selected a box, and tried to start the car. No go. This went on for about ten more people. Then my name was called. My stomach dropped. My hands were shaking. My heart was racing. I somehow managed to make it to the stage without my knees buckling. I went up, shook hands with the sponsors, closed my eyes and prayed my hand would be lead to the right key.

I walked over to the car and got in. A representative from Coca-Cola was in the passenger seat ready to help the sweepers. I put my foot on the clutch. (It was a standard car and the car would not start if the clutch was not depressed even if I had the right key.) I opened the little box and looked at the key. It didn't look like a Mini key. (Was the Classic key different from the standard Cooper and Cooper S keys??) I began to panic. The key wouldn't even go in to the ignition. The representative said she was sorry. If I couldn't get the key in the ignition it wasn't the right key. I didn't win the car.

I got out of the car and was asked to draw the name of the next sweeper. I picked a name from the drum and then turned to go back to my seat. I was so sad, as I walked back to my family. I felt like the biggest loser. I really thought, with all my heart, I was going to win that car. I guess it wasn't meant to be.

We sat in the stands watching to see what would happen. Only about five more names were called before someone started the car. The entire process only lasted about 30 minutes. I realized I was lucky to even have a chance to go up and try because about two-thirds of the contestants didn't even get a chance to pick a key. Also, the young man that won the car didn't even own one. He needed the car more than I did.

I chose to include this particular story because I wanted you to know: 1) I do not win every sweepstakes I enter and 2) I continue to be happy and excited every day about entering sweepstakes, dreaming about the prizes I could win, being and feeling lucky, and just overall passionate about sweeping.

"The only sure thing about luck is that it will change."
Bret Harte

Affidavits and Release Forms

It is important to read the documentation sent to you because you could lose if you do not respond correctly or within the specified period of time. Affidavits and release forms are the legal documents that you and any companions sign stating you agree to, and will abide by, the official sweepstakes rules.

Once, I won a $100 gift certificate and while speaking with the judging agency representative, I discovered my name was the third one drawn. The first two "winners" did not call them back.

TIP: I have had winning notifications arrive by mail the day the release forms are due back at the judging agency or even several days after. Call them immediately; explain your predicament and you will generally get your prize. Everyone understands that occasionally the postal mail takes longer to arrive than originally anticipated.

The time limit to respond will differ from sweepstakes to sweepstakes, so again, **read the rules** to determine how much time you have to reply. Otherwise, you may forfeit the prize.

Due to the specific promotional laws surrounding certain industries (e.g. alcohol, tobacco, etc.) you will get an affidavit for every prize they giveaway, even if it's only worth five dollars. It may seem like a waste of time to you, but they must follow those regulations if they wish to continue offering sweepstakes as part of their marketing programs.

Completing the Forms

Most affidavits and release forms are several pages long and may require a variety of sections to be filled out on each page. It's important to review each page very carefully, ensure you can fulfill all the requirements asked of you (such as paying airport taxes or getting it notarized) and that to complete each and every section; name, address, initials, skill testing question (if required), etc.

If a release is not completed properly or received back in time, you will be disqualified. I have had to disqualify winners in the past. It is not a fun thing to do, but it is legally required on behalf of the sponsor.

TIP: If you do not own a scanner, take a picture of each page and email them back.

STORY: Be sure to budget for, and buy, international rate plans for your cellphone when on vacation. Check several times a day (while staying in in the present moment) for important winning emails, voicemails or texts.

୨୦୧୨

Tamara—Syracuse, NY

While we were away on our 20th wedding anniversary vacation in Cancun, Mexico I was notified through email, twitter, a text, and a call with a voicemail, letting me know I was chosen as the potential grand prizes winner in the *SCANWORKX Operation Sentinel Sweepstakes*. All I had to do was respond back to them (call them and be on the air) within 15 minutes and I would win $10,000 and a Galaxy Tablet!

If we were not on vacation I would have been on top of this, since I am constantly on my laptop, phone, Twitter, etc. and would have received the message. However, being away out of the country we decided not to use our cell phones since it would cost a fortune (unless one of our kids called in an emergency situation).

I did notice the text they sent to let me know I was a potential winner and that I had to call them back to win the $10,000 within 15 minutes. I freaked out and told my husband I didn't care if this call would be expensive or not, that I was making this call!

I had no clue as how to make a call on my phone that was out of the country, so I tried adding a #1 to it, but did not go through because we were in Mexico. I then used the phone in our hotel room and still could not get the call to go through to the U.S. without giving them a credit card. By the time I did get though and let them know who and where I was they said unfortunately they had to pick another winner because I called back 15 minutes past the deadline. Needless to say I cried and cried. I did not want to leave our hotel room to do anything because I was devastated.

This was our anniversary trip so I did get my emotions in check and went out later that day to do something fun, but to this day, I regret not getting back to them in time. They did announced me as their winner on their Twitter feed as well (@ScanWorkX) and thanked me for being a good sport about losing the $10,000.

The ironic part is; two days before we left for our vacation, my husband got into an accident with our car and it was totalled. We had no collision insurance on it, so were in desperate need for a car. The prize would have paid for a car with no payments.

୨୦୧୨

I understand wanting to be present and disconnecting from technology while on vacation. It truly is the healthy thing to do. What I prefer to do is keep my phone with me at all times, as I also use it as my camera, but keep it tucked away in a bag. This way I have it if I get a call or text, but I am not on my phone every five minutes.

When I wrote the first edition of *You Can't Win If You Don't Enter* although the Internet was well established globally, it was very difficult to connect outside of your home or office. It was also expensive to get calls, check voicemail, etc.

Now almost everywhere you go you can find a free WiFi hotspot and most service providers offer inexpensive travel packages for cell service. There is no longer an excuse to miss out on a win because you can't get a call, check voicemail or email.

The only thing you still need to do is have a friend check you mail and doorstep for packages.

Forfeiting a Prize

You entered a contest hoping to win one of the amazing grand prize, however you won one of the many secondary prizes. Should you forfeit the prize hoping to win the grand prize instead?

NEVER FORFEIT A PRIZE! You will not win the grand prize in lieu of a minor prize that you forfeited. Let me explain.

Firstly, I am not only a contestor, but a Contest Manager. I have been conducting drawings for my own giveaways and many clients over the past ten years.

Secondly, the drawings are conducted so a potential winner is selected for each prize, along with back-ups. If you were selected to win a secondary prize, your name may or may not be one of the back-ups for the grand prize. If you forfeit your prize, chances are you will end up with nothing.

My advice would be to keep entering for the prizes you want to win and one day you will be selected as the grand prize winner.

All that said, I do know Americans who have turned down grand prizes due to the tax burden. They originally entered for other prizes, or their circumstances changed between entering and winning, so they had to decline.

Tax Implications?

In the United States, sponsors are under legal obligation to the IRS to file your information as a winner if your prize has a value of more than $600 USD. They will request your SSN (Social Security Number) on the affidavit and you are required to provide it. After all the paperwork is officiated, at the end of the tax year, the sponsor will send you a FORM 1099-MISC for you to include on your next income tax filing. (See chapter, Tax Implications, for additional information.)

In Canada we do not pay taxes on winnings of any kind. (The exception may be if your employer is holding an internal contest. The prize may be considered a taxable employee benefit. Check with your Human Resources and/or Accounting Department.)

I was told of one contest in particular that wanted the winner's SIN (Social Insurance Number) to release the prize. This was a contest run by a US contest management company and assumed the procedure to release a prize was the same in Canada as it was in the US. If you win a prize from the US, you are not required to pay tax or release your SIN.

RESOURCE: For more information regarding Social Security Numbers (SSN) you can access the government anti-fraud facts here: https://www.ssa.gov/antifraudfacts/

RESOURCE: For more information regarding Social Insurance Numbers (SIN), you can access the government fact sheet here: http://bit.ly/SocialInsuranceNumber

No one can withhold a product or service if you refuse to give out your SIN.

Remember, giving out your SIN to an unauthorized party ties in to fraud and scams. DO NOT give out any personal information you are uncomfortable with.

Be aware, if you are a Canadian and win from a US-based contest, you will probably have to pay customs, duties and taxes on the prize when it crosses the border. If an item has a value of more than $20.00 CAD, taxes generally apply. The total amount you have to pay will be determined by the shipping method. Items shipped via courier will have a higher fee because they have customs brokers that clear all items so they can get across the border in a timely manner. Canada Post charges a small fee (approx. $5.00) to clear a package above the taxes owed to the CRA (Canada Revenue Agency).

You can refuse to accept the package and not pay the customs, duties and taxes. The package will be returned to the sender. As a courtesy you should notify the contest management company or sponsor and let them know why you refused the package.

Some prizes may be detained or even refused at the border. Items such as weapons, fresh fruit/vegetables, meat, chemicals, plants, tobacco, and alcohol may face quarantines or might be refused altogether. You may not want to even enter such contests since the prize could be detained or refused at the border.

If you do pay custom charges, you can fill out the form attached to your package (or see link below) and request a reassessment and possible refund. If you enclose a copy of your win notice and a letter stating the item was a win and therefore free, you have a good chance of having the custom charges refunded.

RESOURCE: For more information visit the Canada Revenue Agency's web site at:
http://bit.ly/RefundProgram

Skill Testing Questions

All contests open to Canadian residents must have an element of skill. This requirement is inherently met by skill contests. Other contests usually satisfy this requirement with a mathematical question. Check with your lawyer before you use any other kind of skill. Canadian case law is quite bizarre on what constitutes sufficient skill. For example, identifying the characters in a sitcom or the products in a catalogue would probably not involve sufficient skill. Mathematical skill-testing questions should consist of a 4-part equation (with two- to three-digit numbers) which either follows the order of mathematics (x, $\div$, $+$, $-$) or uses brackets. We do not know how difficult the math must be, but Grade 6 level is probably not enough (unless the contest is aimed at children).

This material has been sourced, with permission, from Chapter 8 of Pritchard, Vogt: *Advertising and Marketing Law in Canada, 4ᵗʰ Edition* **(LexisNexis Canada Inc.) (2012)**

Skill Testing Questions
In Canada, it is considered an illegal lottery to dispose of prizes by chance alone. Some smart advertising lawyers (no doubt) found the "skill" loophole, and the requirement to correctly answer a mathematical skill-testing question to win a sweepstakes or contest became "de rigueur" in Canada.

What is sufficient skill is a matter of some debate. A line of cases that concludes that shooting a turkey from 50 yards is insufficient skill but a mathematical skill-testing question *is* sufficient skill causes most promoters to stick to mathematics.

The Order of Mathematics

Remember in Grade 5 when you learned the order of mathematics (in the absences of brackets) was multiplication, division, addition and subtraction? It is surprising how many promotion houses do not remember this until they receive a complaint from a mathematics professor who claims that the correct answer to the skill question is a negative number, and, therefore, he is the only winner of their contest. Be sure that the question either has brackets or always goes in the correct mathematical order. Also ensure that the answer is a whole number.

This material has been sourced, with permission, from Chapter 22 of Pritchard, Vogt: Advertising and Marketing Law in Canada, 4th Edition (LexisNexis Canada Inc.) (2012)

There is quite a debate amongst my fellow contestors regarding Skill Testing Questions (STQs). Are questions answered calculating left to right or should the order of operations (aka BEDMAS) be used?

e.g. $8 + 2 \times 4$

left-to right = 40 (8 plus 2 equals 10, times 4 equals 40)

BEDMAS = 16 (multiplication always comes before addition, so 2 times 4 equals 8, plus 8 equals sixteen)

If you are using BEDMAS, operations are done in a specific order. This order is as follows:

Simplify all operations inside of parentheses (brackets).

Simplify all exponents, working your way from left to right.

Complete all multiplications and divisions, working your way from left to right.

Complete all additions and subtractions, working your way from left to right.

BEDMAS is defined as:

B – Brackets
E – Exponents
D – Division
M – Multiplication
A – Addition
S – Subtraction

A good STQ will be written in such a way that the answer will be the same either way or will be *written* out.

2 x 4 + 8 = 16

or

Multiply 40 by 2
Add 10
Divide by 2
Subtract 5
Answer = 40

If you get an STQ and are unsure how to answer it, *ask*. If called, I will ask if the question is to be answered left-to-right or using BEDMAS. The sponsors and contest management companies want you to win so they will direct you on how to answer. Most times they will read out one set of operations before going on to the next one.

e.g. Please add 2 and 8. Now multiply by 4. Now minus 10. What's the answer? 30.

NOTE: Sometimes the mathematical operators for multiplication (x) and divide (÷) are shown as a star (*) and a forward slash (/) respectively.

If I receive a set of release forms and are unsure of which formula to use (left-to-right or BEDMAS), I put in both answers explaining why there are two answers and they should fix their STQ. Maybe next time they will create a less confusing STQ. There usually aren't many math majors in the marketing department!

STORY: Fred submitted a very funny story about his wife Betty and her first experience with answering an over-the-phone Skill Testing Question.

৪৩০৪

Fred—Prince George, BC
The wife got her first phone call and skill testing question today. It went something like this: Wife answers phone and runs into computer room, "Fred

I think I won something!" Then talks on the phone, "I had better sit down." CRASH! BANG! OUCH! Picks up phone while lying on floor and says, "I missed the chair." I pick up extension phone and hear a guy laughing so hard he can hardly say the skill testing question. The wife hollers, "Fred have you got the answer?" More laughing. Then she says, "My husband says it's 350." I hear some guy say, "I guess that is right, what is your email address?" Wife says "XXX funny sign XXX dot CA." I hear more laughing and the guy says, "Well you made my day! Did you hurt yourself? You have won an Apple iPod." Wife, "An I what?" "An iPod." says the guy. Wife, "Is that something to do with glasses?" Guy, "I wish I had this on tape." That's when I hung up the extension.

NOTE: Betty's email address was Xed out to protect her privacy.

ಬೊೞೞ

Missing Prizes

What happens if a prize never arrives? You win a fantastic prize; you wait weeks and weeks, and nothing. What do you do?

This is why it is very important to:

1. track all your wins in a spreadsheet
2. and, keep a copy of all your winning correspondence, release forms and affidavits.

On average a prize will take up to eight weeks to arrive. If you have not heard from the sponsor or ad or judging agency *and* you have not received your prize, it's time to follow-up.

Your first course of action will be to contact the person that notified you of your win. Their contact will be on the email or letter. (Hopefully, you got their phone number if you were notified by phone.)

When you ask about the missing prize, be polite. The people running the companies you are dealing with are human. They occasionally make mistakes and are relying on others to get their job done. Many times one email or phone call is all that is required to find out your prize status.

What happens if you are ignored, or the person you are dealing with is rude? Go to their superior. The best person to reach out to is the President or Vice President of Marketing. Action will usually be taken quite quickly because they will want to know why their staff member isn't doing their job.

If you are dealing with an ad or judging agency, you will want to contact the President or Vice President of Marketing of the contest sponsor. The sponsor will want to know why the company they hired to run the contest for them isn't taking care of their customers. Again, action will be taken very quickly.

To find out who the managers or directors of these companies are either:

- use Google,
- or call the company and ask who is in that particular role.

LinkedIn, as its main focus is business, is also a good resource for searching corporate executives.

If you won a contest via social media, or you cannot locate additional sponsor or agency information, you can also post a message on the sponsor's Facebook page or you can tweet them.

If you won a blog contest, and the bloggers is non-responsive, take the above actions with the contest sponsor to receive a satisfactory outcome.

I have received all the big prizes I have won. Most companies are competent and expedient. Only on occasion have I had to take the above actions and received my prize. In all the years I have been sweeping I have never received less than a handful of prizes. The value of those prizes was so small, and the time invested to continue chasing the missing prize, began to outweigh the value. At that point my time was better spent entering new contests.

It's up to you to decide how long and how far you are willing to go to receive what you have won.

"Of course the game is rigged.
Don't let that stop you—
if you don't play, you can't win."
Robert Heinlein

AVOIDING SCAMS

You Never Have To Pay To Receive a
Prize From a Legitimate Sweepstakes!

I cannot stress this enough!

The only money you may have to pay in the United States is the government taxes and in both countries any expenses (specifically for a trip win) not covered by the sponsor. The official rules will specifically state if and what you are responsible for. Generally, it will be all monies you choose to spend (e.g. spending money on a trip or to upgrade a car). The taxes (e.g. airport and hotel) or the customs and duties (due on a prize won in another country being shipped to country of residence. (See chapter, Tax Implications.) Those funds are payable to the federal government, or service you chose to use, and do not go to the sponsor or judging agency.

TIP: When you win a trip, it's a cheap trip--not a free trip. An example of this is when you win the airfare and hotel stay, you are responsible for all other monies spent on the trip: meals, taxis, tours, souvenirs, gratuities, etc. Ensure you budget for vacations if you are entering to win trips.

In twenty plus years of infrequent sweeping and fifteen years of daily sweeping I have only ever had one "winning" phone call asking for my credit card number so I could receive my prize. I told them I knew it was a scam and they promptly hung up. I do get dozens of emails, on a daily basis, informing me I won the lottery in some foreign country. My spam filtering software promptly dumps most of those into my Deleted Folder—that is one way to easily spot a legitimate congratulatory email from a fraudulent one.

TIP: Check your spam folder once per day (and your Other message folder in Facebook) to ensure a legitimate winning email didn't accidently get caught by your anti-spam software.

A legitimate congratulatory call, letter or email will offer you information that 1) you will probably remember (the sweepstakes name) and 2) contact information you can easily verify (e.g. employee, company phone number, address, etc.) If you are unsure, investigate further by doing an Internet search or contacting the company to verify the sweepstakes information.

If you get one of these fraudulent phone calls, emails or letters, get as much information as you can (in the case of a phone call) and forward the information to the authorities.

Many organizations and companies also offer information to help you spot a scam in moments.

The Federal Trade Commission has an online article and a downloadable pamphlet called Prize Offers: You Don't Have To Pay To Play. http://bit.ly/AvoidPrizeScams

The USPS has a webpage devoted to avoiding sweepstakes scams with a downloadable pamphlet called A Consumer's Guide to Sweepstakes and Lotteries along with links to other resources. http://bit.ly/USPSAvoidScams

Let's help end fraud.

The **Internet Crime Complaint Center** (www.ic3.gov) is a partnership between the Federal Bureau of Investigation (FBI) and the National White Collar Crime Center (NW3C). This partnership was created to stop Internet and online fraud including sweepstakes scams.

You can submit your complaint, www.ic3.gov/complaint, or contact the authorities online, www.ic3.gov

Sadly, many telephone scams perpetrated originate in Canada. The RCMP (Royal Canadian Mounted Police), the OPP (Ontario Provincial Police), the Competition Bureau and the Federal Government set up **Canadian Anti-Fraud Centre** (www.antifraudcentre-centreantifraude.ca/index-eng.htm) to stop fraud. This coalition was originally intended to stop telephone scams. Due to the advent of the Internet and the globalization of fraud, they not only try to stop all fraud in Canada but work with the authorities worldwide to stop fraud and catch these con artists globally.

You can report any suspicious activity to CAFC at the same toll free number in the Canada or the United States.
Toll Free: 1-**888-495-8501**
Toll Free Fax Number: 1-**888-654-9426**

If the con-artists are no longer able to dupe people into giving them money, the scams and fraud will stop.

Government Regulations

Sweeping Problems

If you have a problem with a sweepstakes your first course of action is to complain to the judging agency. Most companies are in business to make money. Their objective is to keep their client's customers happy so they will usually do their best to resolve any issues you may have.

The two most common problems you may try to get resolved are problems with the sweepstakes itself (e.g. unclear or conflicting rules, problems with the online entry form, etc.) or when trying to obtain a prize (e.g. the prize is extraordinarily late in arriving, not the prize stated you would receive, etc.)

If you are not satisfied with that resolution, speak to the marketing department of the sponsoring company. The sponsor is paying the judging agency to promote their products and services along with attracting new customers. It's in their best interest to have happy winners of their sweepstakes telling all their friends how wonderful the product or experience was, so usually they will do what they can to solve any problems that come up.

If you are still unsatisfied, the last course of action would be to complain to the government.

Who regulates sweepstakes and games of chance?

Both federal and state governments have jurisdiction over sweepstakes and games of chance.

There are several federal statutes and regulations that prohibit unfair and deceptive acts, activities pertaining to lotteries, and the mailing or broadcasting of certain materials. These laws are enforced primarily by the Federal Trade Commission (FTC), United States Postal Service (USPS), Federal Communications Commission (FCC) and the United States Department of Justice (DOJ).

The states also license and regulate games of chance. All states have statutes prohibiting lotteries, which are generally defined as any promotion requiring all three elements of chance, prize and consideration, unless specifically authorized (for example, state-run lotteries or licensed charitable raffles or bingo).

175

Federal

If you wish to complain about a promotion, you will need to do so through the Federal Trade Commission (FTC) or the United States Postal Service (USPS).

FTC

Toll Free:
1-877-FTC-HELP (1-877-382-4357)

Mailing Address:
Consumer Response Center
600 Pennsylvania Avenue NW
Washington, DC 20580

Online Complaint Form:
www.ftc.gov/ftc/cmplanding.shtm

Contact Us:
www.ftc.gov/ftc/contact.shtm

You can also forward unsolicited commercial email (spam), including phishing messages (see chapter, Play Safe), directly to the FTC at spam@uce.gov. These messages will be stored in a database law enforcement agencies to use in their investigations.

USPS

Toll Free:
1-877-876-2455

Mailing Address:
Criminal Investigations Service Center
Attn: Mail Fraud
22 S. Riverside Plaza, Suite 1250
Chicago, IL 60606-6100

Website:
https://postalinspectors.uspis.gov/

Online Complaint Form:
http://postalinspectors.uspis.gov/forms/MailFraudComplaint.aspx

State

You would want to contact your local state government to obtain permits and licenses if you are interested in holding any type of gaming activity. Many organizations do this (e.g. soccer and hockey clubs, school and church groups, etc.) when they want to raise money for their group or club by holding a raffle, casino night or bingo.

Your state's attorney general is also a place you can go to for assistance if you have a problem with a sweepstakes.

Alabama
www.ago.state.al.us

Alaska
www.law.state.ak.us

Arizona
www.azag.gov

Arkansas
www.ag.arkansas.gov

California
http://oag.ca.gov/

Colorado
www.coloradoattorneygeneral.gov

Connecticut
www.ct.gov/ag

Delaware
http://attorneygeneral.delaware.gov

District of Columbia
http://oag.dc.gov/

Florida
http://myfloridalegal.com

Georgia
http://ganet.org/ago

Hawaii
http://ag.hawaii.gov/

Idaho
www.ag.idaho.gov

Illinois
http://illinoisattorneygeneral.gov

Indiana
www.in.gov/attorneygeneral

Iowa
www.IowaAttorneyGeneral.org

Kansas
http://ag.ks.gov/home

Kentucky
http://ag.ky.gov

Louisiana
www.ag.state.la.us

Maine
www.maine.gov/ag

Maryland
www.oag.state.md.us

Massachusetts
www.mass.gov/ago

Michigan
www.michigan.gov/ag

Minnesota
www.ag.state.mn.us

Mississippi
www.ago.state.ms.us

Missouri
http://ago.mo.gov

Montana
https://dojmt.gov/

Nebraska
http://ago.nebraska.gov/

New Hampshire
http://doj.nh.gov/

New Jersey
www.state.nj.us/lps

New Mexico
www.nmag.gov

New York
www.ag.ny.gov

North Carolina
www.ncdoj.com

North Dakota
www.ag.nd.gov

Ohio
www.ohioattorneygeneral.gov

Oklahoma
www.ok.gov/oag

Oregon
www.doj.state.or.us

Pennsylvania
www.attorneygeneral.gov

Rhode Island
www.riag.state.ri.us

South Carolina
www.scattorneygeneral.org

South Dakota
http://atg.sd.gov/

Tennessee
www.tn.gov/attorneygeneral

Texas
https://texasattorneygeneral.gov/

Utah
http://attorneygeneral.utah.gov

Vermont
www.atg.state.vt.us

Virginia
www.oag.state.va.us

Washington
www.atg.wa.gov

West Virginia
www.ago.wv.gov

Wisconsin
www.doj.state.wi.us

Wyoming
http://ag.wyo.gov/

The National Association of Attorneys General (www.naag.org) members are the Attorneys General of the 50 states and the District of Columbia and the chief legal officers of the Commonwealths of Puerto Rico (Secretary of Justice) and the Northern Mariana Islands, and the territories of American Samoa, Guam, and the Virgin Islands. The U.S. Attorney General is an honorary member.

Who regulates contests and games of chance?

All three levels of government—federal, provincial and municipal—have jurisdiction over contests and games of chance.

The federal government, through Industry Canada, provides information and examines complaints regarding contests, draws and sweepstakes in relation to the promotional contest provision of the Competition Act.

Municipalities also license and regulate games of chance; their jurisdiction is determined largely, but not entirely, by the dollar value of the prizes offered.

The provinces regulate and license all of the activities listed for municipalities when the prizes are large, as well as bingos, fairs and exhibitions.

<u>Federal</u>

If you wish to complain about a promotion, you will need to do so through Industry Canada with the exception of Quebec who must go through the Régie des alcools, des courses et des jeux.

Promotional Contests
Section 74.06 of the *Competition Act* is a civil provision. It prohibits any promotional contest that does not disclose the number and approximate value of prizes, the area or areas to which they relate and any important information relating to the chances of winning such as the odds of winning. It also stipulates that the distribution of prizes cannot be unduly delayed and that participants be selected or prizes distributed on the basis of skill or on a random basis. It should be noted that in addition to complying with section 74.06 of the Act, a contest must be lawful as it relates to other federal statutes such as the *Criminal Code*, as well as other relevant provincial statutes and local by-laws. The possible applicability of these statutes and by-laws should be explored.

If a court determines that a person has engaged in conduct contrary to section 74.06, it may order the person not to engage in such conduct, to publish a corrective notice and/or to pay an administrative monetary penalty of up to $750,000 in the case of a first time occurrence by an individual and $10,000,000 in the case of a first time occurrence by a corporation. For subsequent orders, the penalties increase to a maximum of $1,000,000 in the case of an individual and $15,000,000 in the case of a corporation.

http://bit.ly/CompetitionBureau1

Ensuring Truth in Advertising
The Competition Bureau promotes truth in advertising in the marketplace by discouraging deceptive business practices and by encouraging the provision of sufficient information to enable informed consumer choice.

The Competition Act contains criminal and civil provisions to address false or misleading representations and deceptive marketing practices in promoting the supply or use of a product or any business interest.

Under the criminal provisions, the general provision prohibits all materially false or misleading representations made knowingly or recklessly. Other provisions specifically prohibit deceptive telemarketing, deceptive notices of winning a prize, double ticketing, and schemes of pyramid selling. The multi-level marketing provisions prohibit certain types of representations relating to compensation.

Under the civil provisions, the general provision prohibits all materially false or misleading representations. Other provisions specifically prohibit performance representations that are not based on adequate and proper tests, misleading warranties and guarantees, false or misleading ordinary selling price representations, untrue, misleading or unauthorized use of tests and testimonials, bait and switch selling, and the sale of a product above its advertised price. The promotional contest provisions prohibit contests that do not disclose required information.

The *Consumer Packaging and Labelling Act, Precious Metals Marking Act* and *Textile Labelling Act* are regulatory statutes. They prohibit false or misleading representations in specific sectors, namely prepackaged consumer products, precious metal articles, and consumer textile articles. These laws set out requirements for basic, standardized labelling information, such as bilingual product descriptions, metric measurement declarations and dealer identity, all of which help consumers to make informed choices.

False or misleading representations and deceptive marketing practices can have serious economic consequences, especially when directed toward large audiences or when they take place over a long period of time. They can affect both business competitors who are engaging in honest promotional efforts, and consumers.

http://bit.ly/CompetitionBureau2

Deceptive Notices of Winning a Prize
Section 53 of the *Competition Act* is a criminal provision. It prohibits the sending of a notice that gives the recipient the general impression he or she has won a prize or other benefit and asks or gives the option to pay money or incur a cost in order to obtain the prize or benefit. The provision applies to notices sent by any means, including but not limited to regular or electronic mail. No offence would arise if the recipient actually receives the prize or benefit and the person who sent the notice:

1. provides fair and adequate disclosure of the number and approximate value of prizes or benefits, the area or areas to which they have been allocated, and any fact that materially affects the chances of winning;

2. distributes prizes without unreasonable delay; and

3. selects participants or distributes prizes randomly or on the basis of participants' skill, in any area to which the prizes or benefits have been allocated.

Any person who contravenes section 53 is guilty of an offence and liable to a fine of up to $200,000 and/or imprisonment up to one year on summary conviction, or to fines in the discretion of the court and/or imprisonment up to 14 years upon indictment.

http://bit.ly/CompetitionBureau3

NOTE: Free online Deceptive Prize Notice information
http://bit.ly/CompetitionBureau4

How to File a Complaint
You may request information or submit a complaint against an organization that adopts business practices which may be in

violation with the *Competition Act*, the *Consumer Packaging and Labelling Act*, the *Textile Labelling Act* and the *Precious Metals Marking Act* administered by the Competition Bureau.

If you wish to file a complaint regarding a deceptive business practice, here is what we need to know to help you:

Personal Information:
Tell us about yourself. Please note that the information collected in this section is protected under the *Privacy Act*.

Target of Complaint:
Tell us about the company or organization that you have a complaint against.

Details of Complaint:
Tell us about your complaint. Provide us with detailed information using products and or services supplied, products name and description.

The Bureau is committed to providing excellent client service. Employees of the Bureau's Information Centre are available to respond to your questions, record complaints and direct calls from Monday to Friday, 8:30 to 4:30 p.m., Eastern Standard Time.

You may make a general enquiry electronically regarding any of the laws under the Bureau's jurisdiction using the Competition Bureau On-Line Complaint/Enquiry Form. The form will be sent to the Information Centre where appropriate action will be taken.

The information on the form will be submitted through a secure server that protects confidential Information. Personal Information collected on this form is protected under the *Privacy Act*.

We suggest you use the On-Line Complaint/Enquiry Form to file a complaint. http://bit.ly/CompetitionBureau5

You might prefer to contact the Information Centre by phone or by facsimile.

Monday - Friday, 8:30 a.m. to 4:30 p.m., Eastern Time.
Toll-free: 1 800 348-5358
TDD (for hearing impaired): 1 800 642-3844
Fax: (819) 997-0324

If you chose to mail your complaint, the address is:

Competition Bureau
50 Victoria Street
Gatineau, Quebec
K1A 0C9

http://bit.ly/CompetitionBureau6

Reproduced with the permission of The Minister of Public Works and Government Services, 2009

Provincial

You would want to contact the provincial and municipal governments to obtain permits and licenses if you are interested in holding any type of gaming activity. Many organizations do this (e.g. soccer and hockey clubs, school and church groups, etc.) when they want to raise money for their group or club by holding a raffle, casino night or bingo. Check with your province's regulations as some of these activities are licensed through your local municipality.

Alberta
Gaming and Liquor Commission
http://bit.ly/AlbertaRaffles

British Columbia
Gaming Policy and Enforcement Branch
http://bit.ly/BritishColumbiaRaffles

New Brunswick
Department of Public Safety
http://bit.ly/NewBrunswickRaffles

Newfoundland
Department of Government Services, Lotteries
http://bit.ly/NewfoundlandRaffles

Northwest Territories
Municipal and Community Affairs
http://bit.ly/NorthwestTerritoriesRaffles

Nova Scotia
Alcohol and Gaming Authority
http://bit.ly/NovaScotiaRaffles

Nunavat
Consumer Affairs
http://bit.ly/NunavatRaffles

183

Manitoba
Loquor and Gaming Authority
http://bit.ly/ManitobaRaffles

Ontario
Alcohol and Gaming Commission of Ontario
http://bit.ly/OntarioRaffles

Quebec
Régie des alcools des courses et des jeux
http://bit.ly/QuebecRaffles

Prince Edward Island
Office of the Attorney General
http://bit.ly/PrinceEdwardIslandRaffles

Telemarketers

If you are afraid of being inundated with telemarketing calls after entering many sweepstakes, don't be. Most companies want their customers and prospects to be happy and will not solicit business in this manner. To stop unwanted calls all you need to do is sign up with the National Do Not Call Registry (www.donotcall.gov) in the U.S. or in the National Do Not Call List (http://bit.ly/DoNotCallListRegistry) and you will not be contacted. If however, the odd telemarketing call does come through, do not hang up. At your first opportunity to speak, politely ask they remove you from their call list. They are legally obligated to do so if you request it. If you hang up, they will call you back.

Avoiding Fake Social Media Contests

Sadly, the popularity of social media has also made it a prime platform for unscrupulous, deceitful and fraudulent behaviour.

Companies fall into two categories:

1. large corporate organizations that have large marketing departments and advertising agencies,
2. and, small or medium sized businesses managing their own marketing programs.

You will find the large corporations and advertising agencies run professional promotions (but, there are exceptions). Many of the smaller companies run high-end promotions also, but some flounder which makes their efforts seem 'scammy'.

The trick is to be able to tell the difference between a legitimate social contest that isn't well run or organized and an outright scam.

If you are unsure, go to the main corporate website and use their social links to get to their official page. You can then scroll their feed and see what real sweepstakes they are hosting. You will know instantly if the online post you saw was real or not.

If you still have questions, you can use the Contact Us page on the corporate website to contact the Marketing Department and ask. They are happy to help as they want positive interactions with their prospects and customers. Plus, let them know if you discovered a fake account so they can get it shut down.

Facebook

Anyone can set-up a Facebook Page in moments. What is worse is fraudsters can easily mimic a national brand. The main things you should look out for when a giveaway seems too good to be true are:

- A recently created account.
- An account with a period after the company name.
- No official check mark beside the name, meaning it's not a verified account.
- An insanely low number of LIKEs for a national brand.
- An amazing prize and no other posts.
- No proper corporate details such as: About, Website, Blog, etc.
- The branding doesn't match. Wrong font, image, etc.

You can also join Fake Sweeps, a Facebook group set-up to help fellow sweepers share and avoid scams.
https://www.facebook.com/Fakesweepstakes

Instagram

Instagram is the second most popular platform for scam giveaways. Just like Facebook, anyone can set-up an Instagram account in moments. Unlike Facebook fraudsters don't seem to mimic national brands. Instead they host giveaways to garner Followers. The main things you should look out for when you come across an Instagram contest are:

- A recently created account with an insanely low number of Followers giving away an amazing prize.
- Virtually no other, or very few posts.
- The prize image is a stolen GIF or worse of an opened product.
- No proper details such as: Avatar, Profile or site URL.

- No proper rules for you to follow. (My #1 Tip!)

Twitter & Pinterest

Twitter and Pinterest tend not to host scam giveaways as they don't have mechanisms to capture someone's contact data directly from the site (opposed to Facebook). However, fraudsters can post a link to a fake online contest.

Stopping Scams

Use your common sense and inner voice. If something seems amiss, it usually is. It will also get easier to spot fake ones the more you enter legitimate contests as you will know what real sweepstakes look like.

Help make the hobby better for everyone by reporting every social scam you find to the platform it's found on. Then block it from your feed. The account is generally shut down by the platform fairly quickly. Although it is like a game of Whac-A-Mole. Just as fast as one is shut down, another pops up. Do not stop blocking and reporting because once the fraudsters find their efforts thwarted at every turn, they will slow down to a trickle.

"A person doesn't know how much he has to be thankful for until he has to pay taxes on it."
Unknown

TAX IMPLICATIONS

In the United States, income tax is due on all winnings. Federal income tax law requires you to report the Fair Market Value (FMV) of all sweepstakes and lottery wins and pay the taxes thereby incurred. The amount you will have to pay is based on your total annual income (including such factors as state of residence, filing status, other income, expenses, etc.) for the year the prize is received; the total could be anywhere from 20%-40% of the FMV.

NOTE: The fair market value is the price at which the property (or item) would change hands between a willing buyer and a willing seller, neither being under any compulsion to buy or to sell and both having reasonable knowledge of relevant facts.

It is especially important to look for the prize details and the value given to the prize. You can then determine if you are willing to pay the taxes if you win. If not, do not enter.

In Canada winners are not taxed on their winnings. However, a winner may be required to pay other taxes and fees such as the case with a trip win. The following example is a standard clause commonly found in most rules:

"The winner and his or her travel companion must travel together, will be responsible for all other costs and expenses including transportation to and from the originating airport, travel and medical insurance, travel documentation, airport improvement fees, all taxes, fuel or other surcharges, gratuities, telephone calls, in-room charges and any other expense not explicitly included in the Prize."

I have had to pay the taxes on several of the trips I have won. Sometimes, even if the clause is in the rules, the sponsor will not request payment of any kind. I always let them ask me and if they do, I happily pay it.

If you are not comfortable paying any amount for a trip win, reread the rules before you ask for a cash substitution as you may find a clause similar to this:

"No extensions will be permitted and the Prize cannot be exchanged, transferred or substituted for cash except that travel company/sponsor reserves the right to offer a comparable product in the event of a vacation package cancellation, Act of God or other unforeseen circumstances. The Prize winners shall not be entitled to receive, in cash, certificate or otherwise, the balance of any amount representing the difference of the Prize retail value and actual cost. No frequent flyer miles will be available."

This is why I will state my #1 entry tip once again:

Read The Official Rules *and* Follow Them!

TIP: If you really like the prize, for example, an all-expense paid trip for 10 to Paris, but the taxes would be prohibitive, enter and if you win, you can request the judging agency for a partial disclaimer, e.g. making the trip for two instead of 10.

In the United States if the prize is valued at more than $600, then the judging agency is legally required to send the winner a Form-1099-Misc (frequently referred to as a ten ninety-nine) reporting the FMV of the prize. If the prize is worth less than $600, you may, or may not, get a Form-1099-Misc. You are still legally obligated to report your winnings when you file your taxes whether or not you receive a Form-1099-Misc. Besides helping you to feel lucky, (see chapter, Attracting Luck) for tax purposes, it is important to track all your wins, and expenses, in a spreadsheet or a software package. (See section, Sweeping Software.)

NOTE: To ensure you only pay FMV on your prizes and your taxes are filed properly, consult your local tax specialist or certified public accountant (CPA). They can also give you advice on your specific tax questions.

To ensure you do not potentially overpay taxes on a prize, document everything associated with that prize. For example, if you win a big screen TV and you receive a Form-1099-Misc stating its value is $5,000, yet the same week you receive the TV you see it advertised in the local paper for $4,000, you would then show an adjustment in your tax return to reflect the difference and the FMV.

TIP: Always get receipts. If required, they can be used to prove to the IRS that a prize's value is lower than the issued Form-1099-Misc saving you tax dollars.

Some Americans choose to treat sweepstaking as a "business" and subject themselves to self-employment taxes. Most sweepers report income and claim deductions as an "activities engaged in for profit." In the latter situation, the taxpayer must itemize deductions and is only allowed to deduct most miscellaneous deductions (which include sweepstaking expenses) to the extent those expenses exceed 2% of the taxpayer's adjusted gross income for the year. If the activity is classified as a "hobby", because it fails to make a profit in enough years, deductions are allowed only to the extent that there is income from sweepstaking in that year. For example, if you only win $1,000 in prizes for the year, but spent $2,000 entering, you cannot claim a loss of $1,000; however you can cancel out your tax liability for the $1,000 in prizes you won.

Expenses can be such things as postage, envelopes, paper and cards, pens, markers, stickers, etc. You may be able to deduct part of your home computer, your Internet access or your text messaging package on your cell phone. Again, I recommend you speak to your CPA to ensure your deductions are allowable, accurate and do not flag you for an audit.

TIP: Get in the habit of asking for and keeping all your receipts.

It is also your responsibility to pay your estimated taxes, especially on large prizes. If you win a car in January, the judging agency may not send you your Form-1099-Misc until the following January. You are required to estimate how much tax you will be paying on the income of the car and make four payments that year (by April 15th, June 15th, September 15th and January 15th). Failure to pay the estimated taxes can result in a penalty in the form of a high interest rate. You could also experience quite a shock at tax time if you must pay a large sum all at once.

NOTE: Prizes are usually non-transferable. This means the one who wins it, is the one that must accept the prize and the one whose name will be on the Form-109-Misc. This is especially important to note if you are entering to win trips, as the one who wins, must go and can take whomever they wish to accompany them. If they cannot travel then the prize is forfeited.

Internal Revenue Service

You can call the Internal Revenue Service (IRS) directly at *1-800-829-1040* or check their website for further resources.
www.irs.gov/individuals/index.html

Sample Form-1099-Misc
http://bit.ly/SampleMISC1099

Estimated Tax Form – 1040ES
http://bit.ly/EstimatedForm

When you receive a Form-1099-Misc, Box 3 should be selected indicating to the IRS you are reporting your win as 'other income'. If Box 7 is checked, 'non-employee compensation', contact the judging agency to get a corrected form.

If you enjoy gambling or buying lottery tickets in addition to sweeping, be aware the wins and losses from gambling must be reported separately on your return.

Information on a W-2G - Sweepstakes, Wagering Pools, and Lotteries
http://bit.ly/InfoW2G

Gambling Winning Form – W2-G
http://bit.ly/FormW2G

Saving to Pay the Taxes

There are a few ways you can save or earn money to help pay the taxes on your winnings:

- Work overtime or get a second job. This option has its own tax implications.
- If the prize is very large such as a car or a house, you can approach your bank for a loan or mortgage, using the prize as collateral.
- Sell some of your tangible prizes (electronics, vehicles) to pay for the taxes on intangible prizes (trips).
- Save your pennies. Some people only spend bills and save all of their change. You would be amazed at how quickly pennies, nickels, dimes and quarters add up to real dollars.

David Bach, author of Automatic Millionaire, coined the term The Latte Factor®. The concept is, if you save the money you normally spend on lattes, bottled water, cigarettes, magazines, fast food, etc. you can change your life. Using David's methods, you can easily save enough money to pay any taxes on any prize you win.

You can read more about his ideas and calculate your Latte Factor here: http://davidbach.com/latte-factor/ or download his app.

"Few people realize that luck is created."
Robert Kiyosaki

ATTRACTING LUCK

As I participated in online forums, attended club meetings and met a multitude of sweepers, I noticed that some people seemed to win far more than others did. What set those people apart? I realized there were seven traits and actions winners possessed and took. They:

1. Think positively.
2. Expect to win.
3. Feel like a winner.
4. Have good chi flowing inside and out.
5. Share with others.
6. Don't cheat.
7. Enter, Enter, Enter...

"Whether you think you can, or you think you can't, you're right."
Henry Ford

Positive Thinking

What is your internal dialogue? Is it positive or negative? Are you always saying, **I can** or, **I can't**? Did you know you choose how you talk to yourself? I have met sweepers that say *"I never win"* or *"I am not lucky"* and I think *"WOW! If you think that way, you definitely won't win."*

Change your internal and external dialogue. Use I am, I can and I will. Speak in the present tense as if it has already happened: "I am lucky." "I am a winner." "I enter as often as I can." "I win often." Pretty soon you will find those statements and beliefs coming true, not only when you sweep, but in all aspects of your life.

WHO DECIDES WHETHER you shall be happy or unhappy? The answer—you do!

A television celebrity had as a guest on his program an aged man. And he was a very rare old man indeed. His remarks were entirely unpremeditated and of course absolutely unrehearsed.

191

They simply bubbled up out of a personality that was radiant and happy. And whenever he said anything, it was so naive, so apt, that the audience roared with laughter. They loved him. The celebrity was impressed, and enjoyed it with the others.

Finally he asked the old man why he was so happy. "You must have a wonderful secret of happiness," he suggested.

"No," replied the old man, "I haven't any great secret. It's just as plain as the nose on your face. When I get up in the morning," he explained, "I have two choices—either to be happy or to be unhappy, and what do you think I do? I just choose to be happy, and that's all there is to it."

That may seem an oversimplification, and it may appear that the old man was superficial, but I recall that Abraham Lincoln, whom nobody could accuse of being superficial, said that people were just about as happy as they made up their minds to be. You can be unhappy if you want to be. It is the easiest thing in the world to accomplish. Just choose unhappiness. Go around telling yourself that things aren't going well, that nothing is satisfactory, and you can be quite sure of being unhappy. But say to yourself, "Things are going nicely. Life is good. I choose happiness," and you can be quite certain of having your choice.

The happiness habit is developed by simply practicing happy thinking. Make a mental list of happy thoughts and pass them through your mind several times every day. If an unhappiness thought should enter your mind, immediately stop, consciously eject it, and substitute a happiness thought. Every morning before arising, lie relaxed in bed and deliberately drop happy thoughts into your conscious mind. Let a series of pictures pass across your mind of each happy experience you expect to have during the day. Savor their joy. Such thoughts will help cause events to turn out that way. Do not affirm that things will not go well that day. By merely saying that, you can actually help to make it so. You will draw to yourself every factor, large and small, that will contribute to unhappy conditions. As a result, you will find yourself asking, "Why does everything go badly for me? What is the matter with everything?"

The reason can be directly traced to the manner in which you begin the day in your thoughts.

Tomorrow try this plan instead. When you arise, say out loud three times this one sentence, "This is the day which the Lord hath made; we will rejoice and be glad in it." (Psalm 118:24) Only personalize it and say, "I will rejoice and be glad in it." Repeat it in a strong, clear voice and with positive tone and emphasis. The statement, of course, is from the Bible and it is a good cure for unhappiness. If you repeat that one sentence three times before breakfast and meditate on the meaning of the words you will change the character of the day by starting off with a happiness psychology.

While dressing or shaving or getting breakfast, say aloud a few such remarks as the following, "I believe this is going to be a wonderful day. I believe I can successfully handle all problems that will arise today. I feel good physically, mentally, emotionally. It is wonderful to be alive. I am grateful for all that I have had, for all that I now have, and for all that I shall have. Things aren't going to fall apart. God is here and He is with me and He will see me through. I thank God for every good thing."

Reprinted with the permission of Scribner, an imprint of Simon & Schuster Adult Publishing Group, from THE POWER OF POSITIVE THINKING by Norman Vincent Peale. Copyright © 1952, 1956 by Prentice-Hall, Inc.: copyright renewed © 1980, 1984 by Norman Vincent Peale. All Rights Reserved

RESOURCE: Anthony Meindl's specialty is getting you to see life from a new perspective. He is the author of At the Left Brain Turn Right and Alphabet Soup for Grown-ups. Check out his weekly video lessons at www.youtube.com/anthonymeindl.

"Luck affects everything; let your hook always be cast. In the stream where you least expect it, there will be fish."
Ovid

Expectations

Do you expect to win? I do. If I go to bed at night and I have not won anything that day I am genuinely disappointed. I am the only person I know that looks forward to Mondays because the judging agencies generally only notify winners during the work week and I can hardly wait for the next winning call, letter or email.

NOTE: We have only once been notified by a judging agency of a win on a Saturday. We have also won online instant win sweepstakes at night or on weekends.

One of Richard Wiseman's four scientific principles of luck is: Expect Good Fortune.

> My research revealed that lucky people do not achieve their dreams and ambitions purely by chance. Nor does fate conspire to prevent unlucky people from obtaining what they want. Instead, lucky and unlucky people achieve, or fail to achieve, their ambitions because of a fundamental difference in how they think about both themselves and their lives.
>
> Earlier on in the book we met lucky competition winners Lynne, Joe and Wendy. All of them won a huge number of prizes, and all put much of their good luck down to the fact that they enter a large number of competitions. As Joe said, "You have to be in to win." Many of the unlucky people explained that they never entered competitions and lotteries because they were convinced that their bad luck would prevent them from winning. As Lucy, a 23-year-old unlucky student, told me:
>
> I can remember, even when I was little, not entering things because I just never won anything. When I was seven, I was at primary school in an assembly and my parents were in the audience. My mum had entered a competition for me and they called out the winner and it was me. But I hadn't entered it, it was my mum. The way I see it, I hadn't won, she had.
>
> Clearly, unlucky people's expectations about competitions are very likely to become self-fulfilling prophecies. By not entering competitions, they severely reduce their chances of winning, and exactly the same attitude affects many important areas of their life. The resulting lack of any attempt to change their lives can easily turn unlucky people's low expectations about the future into a miserable reality.

From THE LUCK FACTOR by Dr. Richard Wiseman. Copyright © 2003 Dr. Richard Wiseman. By permission of Hachette Books, a division of Hachette Book Group, Inc. All rights reserved.

RESOURCE: You can get a FREE The Luck Factor PDF, written by Dr. Richard Wiseman, highlighting the main points of his study. http://bit.ly/TheLuckFactor

STORY: Sometimes you just <u>know</u> you are going to win.

ℰℭ

Sharon—Aurora, ON

Several years ago a local radio station was running a text-in-to-win contest. It was run over a weekend and you could instantly win a trip to Cuba. To enter you had to text a message to the station at 1:30pm and they would call back the winner. They were running it once on Saturday and once on Sunday. I had a premonition I was going to win. I could feel it. I just knew. Saturday I didn't win. On Sunday I had a client from 1:00-2:00pm, so I got my phone message set-up and ready to go, then slid my phone in my smock. I even told my client I was going to win a trip that day. I was doing a massage and could not use my phone. I couldn't have the radio on in the treatment room either, as we played relaxing music. So at 1:30pm I just hit send. I had to put the phone on silent too. For the entire second half of the treatment I could feel the phone vibrating in my pocket. As soon as my client left I called the station back to claim my prize. The announcer said that she believes if you win you win. I'm glad she didn't give it to someone else when it took me a half hour to call back. Cuba was great!

ℰℭ

"You get what you think about,
whether you want it or not"
Abraham

The Law of Attraction

In 2003 a colleague introduced the concept of the Law of Attraction to me. I found the idea a bit odd at first and the more I read, the more I liked the notion that I could be lucky and be a winner by feeling lucky and feeling like a winner. Since then the book and movie The Secret have made the Law of Attraction a household term.

"We create by feeling, not by thought!"
Lynn Grabhorn

The Law of Attraction is a powerful universal law. It affects every part of your life. It is the secret to being happy, living a successful fulfilling life, and having the ability to get what you want.

Your understanding of and application of the Law of Attraction relates directly to the quality of your life, your wealth and abundance (or lack thereof) and your degree of success.

Many people measure only one dimension of success: money or wealth. However, real success is much more holistic and includes: financial success; relationship success; career and fulfilment success; physical health and well-being; and spiritual success. The Law of Attraction plays a major role in each of these areas!

The Law of Attraction simply states: "You attract into your life whatever you give your attention, focus, and energy to." This is true whether what you attract is wanted or unwanted.

Think of yourself as a large magnet. On that magnet is a control dial, which has settings ranging from crappy to wonderful. Whatever the dial is set for, that is what comes into your life. The dial setting determines the opportunities, the people, the events, the circumstances and the coincidences that show up in your life.

Let us make this analogy a little bit more complex. Think of yourself again as that large magnet but instead of one dial there are many dials. These dials have labels; relationships, money, happiness, health and well-being, career, and so on. It is very possible to have one dial set on wonderful and another set on crappy. All you have to do to see this is look around. You will see people with one part of their life working and another part not working. Said another way, you will see people getting what they want in one area of their life and not in another.

You are that magnet! Your thoughts and feelings, and especially your habitual thoughts and feelings, determine the settings of your dials. If you think crappy thoughts and feel crappy feelings you will attract a crappy life. If you think wonderful thoughts and feel wonderful feelings you will attract a wonderful life. It really can be that simple. Unfortunately, we human beings love to make it much more difficult.

At an energy level here is how that looks:

According to quantum physics, absolutely everything is energy. You are energy. The chair you are sitting on is energy. Your clothes are energy. Your thoughts are energy and so are your feelings.

The concept that "everything is energy" is contrary to our experience. We think we are solid. We think the chair we are sitting on is solid and so on. So, it is important for you to make this leap and keep in mind the fact everything is energy.

Energy vibrates, and different qualities of energy vibrate at different rates. Energies that are on the same frequency attract each other. They are in a state of resonance. Energies that are on different frequencies repel each other.

Your thoughts and feelings are energy. The energy from your thoughts and feelings penetrates both time and space and in the process attracts and repels. They attract similar energies and they repel dis-similar energies. These energies take the form of people, events, circumstances and coincidences.

Contrary to most people's opinion, getting what you want has very little to do with being worthy, deserving or even earning it. Getting what you want is a matter of you vibrating at the same frequency as that which you wish to attract into your life.

Reprinted with the permission of Jonathan Manske LLC, www.JonathanManske.com, from The Law of Attraction Made Simple by Jonathan Manske. Copyright © 2008

"The Law of Attraction does not respond to the words you use or the thoughts you think. It simply responds to how you feel about what you say and what you think."
Michael Losier

There are some actions you can take to begin vibrating to attract what you do want, as opposed to what you don't want.

SELF TALK
A Self Talk is an expression we use as a statement of truth. It can be positive or negative and it often made unconsciously. It can also be called your inner voice.

Negative Self Talk

- I'll have to work hard to make good money.
- I never win the lottery.

- I'll never lose the weight I want.
- Good women/men are hard to find.
- Money comes in one hand and goes out the other.
- It's hard to get clients during the summer.
- I take one step forward and two steps back.
- My business slows down during the holidays.

Complaining and worrying are negative statements. Every time you complain about something, you're giving more attention to what you don't like. When you worry about the future, you're giving more attention to what you don't want.

Positive Self Talk
- I'm lucky, because I always find money.
- I always find work and clients easily.
- Everything I touch turns to gold.
- I make friends easily.
- Money comes to me at the right time.
- I always get a great parking spot.

At this point, you're probably asking yourself how you can stop your pattern of negative thinking. The answer comes in the act of rephrasing what you think and what you say.

HOW TO REPHRASE NEGATIVE SELF TALK
As you become more aware of your use of language and its importance in your vibration, you will begin to catch yourself whenever you make a negative statement. When you hear it, turn the negative into a positive by restating what you have just said. Preface your sentence with "in the past." For example, if you hear yourself say, "It's hard to find clients," rephrase it by saying, "In the past, it was hard to find clients."

Copyright ©2003 by Michael Losier. Used by permission.
www.michaellosier.com or www.lawofattractionbook.com

RESOURCE: Michael Losier hosts a weekly online video class on the Law of Attraction (LOA) called Hangout With Michael. www.hangoutwithmichael.com

STORY: Carmen shows us how she used the Law of Attraction in her life to attract wins. The trick is to do all three steps: Ask, Believe and Receive. Most people only do the first two.

Carmen—Norfolk, VA

I'd like to tell you about how The Secret worked for me in sweepstakes and other aspects of my life.

In 2004 my life changed. My husband had been out of work for about a year and a half. We had been married for 20 years, everything we owned we got when we first got married and it all was in need of repair or needed to be replaced. Money was tight. I had tried part-time jobs that were getting me nowhere.

I knew I had to stop the negative thinking and find a solution. I started thinking maybe I can win the things I need, so I started entering mail-in sweepstakes. I treated it like my part-time job. I spent 2-4 hours every evening looking for sweepstakes for the things I "needed" like a new washer.

At first I had thoughts like, "This isn't going to work, and I'm just wasting needed money on stamps." Then I would say to myself, "I need help, this will be worth it." After the first month I won a $50 gift card for a department store. A few months went by and nothing. The washer was squeaking louder! The truck needed new tires. What was I going to do? I started to worry again but I changed my thinking to, "I need help and this is how I will get it." and "Investing money in stamps will pay off."

On Christmas Eve I was baking cookies and I couldn't get the oven door to close. Frustrated I remember saying to myself, "Great! Something else we need to replace. Where is the money going to come from? I need help and I need it NOW!"

Then an amazing thing happened. Not more than two minutes later, the UPS truck showed up at my door with a letter stating I had won a $14,000 shopping spree at Sears and a check for $4100 to pay the taxes! What an awesome prize!!

My positive thinking and persistence paid off!! I told the Universe what I needed instead of complaining and feeling sorry for myself and look what happened! I got every appliance replaced, new tires for the truck, new prescription glasses, everything I "needed" and more. I was even able to help other people which made me feel so good. The Law of Attraction truly works. I'm a believer!

I have continued my positive thinking and have won some unbelievable prizes for myself, family and friends. What a great feeling to surprise someone with a prize they didn't expect.

෩ඏ

TIP: Keep a memory box and/or a spreadsheet of all your wins. I have a memory box that I keep all the affidavits, congratulatory letters, ticket stubs, pictures, etc. in. I also keep a spreadsheet tracking all of our wins. Whenever I feel we are having a "dry" spell, I pull out the box or look at the spreadsheet and I instantly feel happy and lucky.

"Be aware of wonder. Live a balanced life—learn some and think some and draw and paint and sing and dance and play and work every day some."
Robert Fulghum

Energy Balancing: Inside & Out

qi (ch$\overline{e}$)

n. the circulating life energy that in Chinese philosophy is thought to be inherent in all things; in traditional Chinese medicine the balance of negative and positive forms in the body is believed to be essential for good health.

Qi in *English* is often spelled as **chi** or **ch'i**. The Japanese form is **ki**.

Chi is a fundamental concept of everyday *Chinese* culture, most often defined as "air" or "breath" (for example, the colloquial *Mandarin* Chinese term for "weather" is tiān qi, or the "breath of heaven") and, by extension, "life force" or "spiritual energy" that is part of everything that exists. References to chi or similar philosophical concepts as a type of *metaphysical* energy that sustains living beings are used in many belief systems, especially in *Asia*.

The chi is what needs to be in perfect balance within and around us to not only attract winnings but to have a joyous and prosperous life. I feel this is what has helped me get to where I am today, not only with contesting, but in life.

There are many ways to balance our inner and outer lives; meditation, visualization, yoga, tai chi, acupuncture, massage, reiki, and Feng Shui. This is a very short list of the types of activities and practices you can participate in to balance your life, your body, your family, your home, YOU.

Most of these balancing activities and practices have been around, within different cultures, for thousands of years. Many are becoming "mainstream" as our modern culture begins to incorporate ancient customs into our daily lives.

There are hundreds of books and websites that discuss each of these activities, practices and more in great detail. I will give you a very brief overview on two topics: 1) Feng Shui, for balancing the outside and 2) chakras, for balancing the inside. There are further resources to be found on my website, at your local bookstore and on the Internet.

Outside

Feng Shui: The art of studying the environment and how energies interact with a home or premise. Feng Shui can hasten fulfillment of a good destiny and give a better quality to life.

THE POWER OF PLACE

Whether we choose to believe it or not, we are greatly affected and influenced, for better or for worse, by our surroundings; particularly the atmosphere and layout of our homes. Not only how we feel, but also how we interact with others, how productive we are, and our resulting life experiences are directly related to our environment. Have you ever visited someone's home or office for the first time and for some strange reason felt out of sorts, ill at ease or just plain anxious while being there? Or had the opposite reaction, felt so wonderful you didn't want to leave? We have all instinctively shared these experiences at one time or another. What we are sensing is the energy or Feng Shui of that place.

Developed over 3,000 years ago in the East, Feng Shui is widely practiced as the science and art of spatial design and object placement which balances and enhances the energy of one's surroundings. This ancient discipline seeks to create harmonious living and working environments to help one achieve optimal health of body, mind and soul. Feng Shui, (pronounced fung shway) are the Chinese words for wind and water, the two greatest forces of nature. It represents the universal energy which flows between heaven and earth, running through and connecting all things.

The Chi in your body acts very similarly to the way the energy in a magnet works; it draws to it and attracts the same type of energy it magnetizes out. If your Chi is sending out energy signals that resonate to a sense of harmony, balance and well-being, then it will draw in the things, events and opportunities that will reflect that feeling. It is so important to realize and remember that all the things that you surround yourself with on a daily basis affect the way Chi flows throughout your home. If positive energy is allowed to flow freely through your environment, then the people who live and work there prosper and benefit.

It is a well-known fact that everything in the world has its origins in the world of energy. Quantum physics now confirms that everything in our universe is made up of a mass of constantly moving energy. All physical matter, no matter how solid it feels, is in fact, only energy vibrating. Thus everything on this planet is interconnected by the vibrations of life-force energy which flows between them. Even in the empty spaces that we cannot see, energy exists as well. This means that our home, too, is composed of energy; it is not separate from us, but is a direct reflection of who we are, reflecting our inner energy and intentions throughout our lives. The vibrations found in your home can either be life-suppressing or life-enhancing and the primary focus of a Feng Shui practitioner is to assist the home owner in creating an environment that supports and nurtures them in all areas of their life, both mentally and physically. Enhancing and harmonizing the Chi of our environment strengthens and enhances our own personal Chi. This in turn produces the three most sought after attributes of a good life: health, wealth and happiness. It is not a magic bullet or a quick fix; it is simply a method, an important tool that can help us address and deal with all of life's issues. It simply suggests that it is much easier to "go with the flow" rather than to constantly struggle upstream against it.

Just as there are several different schools of martial arts, so to, in the world of Feng Shui. Black Sect Feng Shui is the most recent school of Feng Shui to be introduced to the West and derives in part from Tibetan Buddhism, as taught be Professor Thomas Lin Yun of Berkeley, California. This school of Feng Shui works purposefully and directly with subtle energy systems within your environment in order to create balance and dynamic life change. This approach is multi-disciplined, incorporating psychology, ecology, interior design, color therapy, yin/yang theory, five element theory, common sense and intuition. By using a more holistic approach in all areas of one's life, Black Sect Feng Shui is a truly unique and powerful art in assisting an individual to make positive life changes. An integral part of improving the Feng Shui of a location is the use of the Bagua. For centuries, the Chinese have placed this mystical energy grid on plots of land, houses and rooms to determine the energy characteristics of an environment. The Bagua is basically a map of the eight major life areas that a person can choose to enhance and strengthen—career, knowledge, family, wealth, fame, love and marriage, children and creativity, and helpful people and support.

To locate these areas the Bagua is superimposed like a template or grid over the floor plan of a home, and even on some specific rooms such as a home office and master bedroom, to indicate the drawbacks and benefits of the location and effects on one's life. During a consultation, the practitioner will be suggesting several different remedies and solutions to a client to attract and enhance a positive flow of Chi throughout the home.

NOTE: Got to http://bit.ly/FengShuiBaguaMap for further Bagua details and a printable map.

Have you ever wondered if you can use Feng Shui principles to increase your luck to help you win sweepstakes? Well, the answer is definitely YES! By implementing just a few easy cures, you can start to energize your space, free up blocked energy and allow the flow of positive energy bringing more luck into your home and life.

Here are just a few easy solutions that you can start to use today.

Clear out the clutter: All the Feng Shui cures and adjustments in the world cannot override the negative effects of clutter. This is the first and most important step to take when trying to improve the energy of your home or workspace. Clutter can be defined as things which are untidy or disorganized, too many things in too small a space, and anything left unfinished. The more of it you have, the more stagnant energy it attracts to itself. This can be one of the biggest and most serious drains of energy in one's life. Consider the stress you feel by facing a cluttered and disorganized desktop. When you clear your workspace, you also clear your head and become better organized and less stressed. This allows for new possibilities, ideas and creative solutions to enter.

Seek ease and comfort: Design your desk, or sweeping area, so everything you need is easily accessible by turning around in your chair or by reaching across the desktop. And don't forget that comfortable chair with a high back for greater support physically and energetically! Since most of us spend hours in front of a monitor, it's so important to be as comfortable as possible to avoid strain and back ache. This will greatly improve your own personal Chi level.

Don't skimp on lighting: Make sure you have adequate lighting and position your light source so it does not create any harsh shadows on your desk. Right-handed people should direct the light over their left shoulder and lefties over their right shoulder for optimum efficiency. If space permits, and it fits in with your decor scheme, treat yourself to a beautiful desktop lamp. Whenever possible try to use full spectrum lighting which imitates the full spectrum of natural sunlight. This newer form of lighting is becoming more main stream as people are looking for more ways to boost their energy and improve their health.

Sit in the power position: Never sit at your desk with your back to the door as this will drain your energy and can make you feel like being stuck in a powerless position. If this situation can't be avoided, place or hang a small mirror in front of you to reflect the door so you can always see someone entering the room. Being startled from behind creates stress and insecurity. If possible, try to have a solid wall behind your chair as this represents more support in your life. If it's impossible to sit in this position, at least use a high back chair.

Plant life: Another great and easy to install cure is plants. Be creative, if space allows, by placing a large beautiful plant or a group of plants in an empty corner. Life attracts positive energy into a space. And don't forget to add a touch of color to your desk by adding a blooming plant or a vase of fresh cut flowers. To attract more wealth, try using a Chinese "money tree" or a vase with eight stalks of bamboo. Eight is the number that represents wealth and prosperity.

Color: Last but not least, and one of the most overlooked cures is the use of color. All colors from soft pastel shades or rich vibrant bold colors can be included in your decor in small or large amounts. The colors we surround ourselves on a daily basis have a great effect on how we feel. Try experimenting with the color of your walls and go with your instinct, using ones that are your favorite. Try bringing in small splashes of color in your accessories. Look at the color of the artwork on your walls. Maybe it's time for a change? Remember; only buy art that you absolutely love. This will work best on enhancing your own personal energy. It's important to realize that it's not how much you spend on the accessory or how large it is. It's the "intention" you place behind it when you purchase it and again when you install it. Remember, where intention goes, energy flows!

Wherever in your home or workplace you choose to use Feng Shui, you can positively enhance your health, wealth, happiness, and luck. How you enhance and nurture your physical environment will determine how your environment will support and sustain your body, mind, and spirit. May the good Chi be with you.

Katherine and Russ Loader, owners of Power of Place, are experts at translating the complex principles of Feng Shui into a language which we can all understand and readily apply to our homes and businesses. www.powerofplace.com

"What we call luck is the inner man externalized. We make things happen to us."
Robertson Davies

Inside

The 7 Chakras – A Beginners Guide To Your Energy System

What on Earth is a Chakra?

In many spiritual and healing disciplines, and in the world of complementary medicine the word Chakra pops up quite a bit. That's fine if you know it means; not so great, and I must say pretty confusing, if you don't. Here's our simple summary of what a Chakra is, and what the Chakra System is all about?

The 7 Chakras are the energy centers in our body in which energy flows through.

The word 'chakra' is derived from the sanskrit word meaning 'wheel'. Literally translated from the Hindi it means 'Wheel of spinning Energy'. A chakra is like a whirling, vortex like, powerhouse of energy. Within our bodies you have seven of these major energy centers and many more minor ones.

You can think of chakras as invisible, rechargeable batteries.

They are charged and recharged through contact with the stream of cosmic energy in the atmosphere in much the same way that your home is connected to a central power source within a city – the only difference is that this cosmic energy source is free.

Imagine this, a vertical power current rather like a fluorescent tube that runs up and down the spine, from the top of the head to the base of the spine. Think of this as your main source of energy. The seven major chakras are in the center of the body and are aligned with this vertical "power line."

Chakras connect your spiritual bodies to your physical one.

They regulate the flow of energy throughout the electrical network (meridians) that runs through the physical body. The body's electrical system resembles the wiring in a house. It allows electrical current to be sent to every part, and is ready for use when needed.

Sometimes chakras become blocked because of stress, emotional or physical problems. If the body's 'energy system' cannot flow freely it is likely that problems will occur. The consequence of irregular energy flow may result in physical illness and discomfort or a sense of being mentally and emotionally out of balance.

Reprinted with the permission of the author; Maya Mendoza. www.zenlama.com

RESOURCE: Caroline Myss has an online Flash-based presentation with good descriptions of what each chakra is and what it relates to. http://bit.ly/YourChakras

7 Awesome Affirmations to Balance Your Chakras
Using the power of affirmations is one of the most effective ways to balance our chakras. Our thoughts create our reality, and by regularly practicing positive chakra balancing affirmations, we can achieve astonishing results in our lives.

Chakra is a Sanskrit word which literally translates into a spinning wheel. According to ancient yogic traditions, there are seven major chakras or energy centers in our body. Each of these chakras corresponds to a particular color-coded vibrational frequency in the universe which influences our physical, emotional and spiritual well-being. When our chakras are perfectly aligned with the universal flow of energy, every aspect of our life becomes harmonious and joyful. We reclaim perfect health, and our love and passion for life becomes renewed.

When using the following affirmations, sit or lie down in a quiet place and focus on the location of each chakra. As you speak out or silently meditate on each affirmation, visualize a wheel spinning face-up in a clockwise direction in the specific color frequency of each chakra.

1. Root Chakra – The root chakra is located at the base of our spine and corresponds to the color red. This chakra relates to our basic human instinct for survival, security and stability.

Affirmation: "I am a divine being of light, and I am peaceful, protected and secure"

2. Sacral Chakra – The sacral chakra is located just below our navel in our lower abdominal region. The color of this chakra is a deep, saturated orange and relates to reproduction on a physical level, creativity and joy and relationships on an emotional level and our energy and passions on a spiritual level.

Affirmation: "I am radiant, beautiful and strong and enjoy a healthy and passionate life"

3. Solar Plexus Chakra – This chakra is located above our navel and directly in our stomach area. The solar plexus chakra therefore plays a vital role in digestion and glows in a bright yellow color. This chakra deals with growth and pertains to issues of the intellect, personal power, control and spiritual evolution.

Affirmation: "I am positively empowered and successful in all my ventures"

4. Heart Chakra – The heart chakra is located in the center of the chest and spins with the vibrant green color of spring. This chakra is one of the most important meditation tools for cleansing and clearing spiritual imbalances. The key issues related to the heart chakra are unconditional love, compassion and wellbeing.

Affirmation: "Love is the answer to everything in life, and I give and receive love effortlessly and unconditionally"

5. Throat Chakra – This chakra is centered in our throat and exudes a pale blue light. The throat chakra governs our ability to express and communicate clear thoughts and ideas. It is also related to truth, maturity, independence and the ability to trust others.

Affirmation: "My thoughts are positive, and I always express myself truthfully and clearly"

6. Third Eye Chakra – The third eye chakra is positioned in the center of our forehead, between our eyebrows. Also known as the brow chakra, it spins in a deep saturated dark blue hue and helps us tap into our inner guidance and divine vision. This chakra deals with developing intuitive clarity, releasing repressed emotions and attaining self-realization.

Affirmation: "I am tuned into the divine universal wisdom and always understand the true meaning of life situations"

7. Crown Chakra – The crown chakra is located at the top of our head or in the crown area and corresponds to the violet color. The role of this chakra is based in awakening consciousness and attaining enlightenment through the integration of the self into the one universal form of intelligence.

Affirmation: "I am complete and one with the divine energy"

Chakra balancing affirmations can create extraordinary revolutions in our spiritual healing journey. There can be nothing more effective and transformative than using your very own power of thought to bring positive changes in your body, mind and soul.

Reprinted with the permission of the author; Sohini Trehan. www.mindbodygreen.com

"The universe operates through dynamic exchange…giving and receiving are different aspects of the flow of energy in the universe. And in our willingness to give that which we seek, we keep the abundance of the universe circulating in our lives."
Deepak Chopra

You Get What You Give

It is my personal observation that the people that post the most contests, help others with answers and in general, share, seem to post the most wins. This principle goes back thousands of years. (See chapter, Join a Sweeping Club.)

Deepak Chopra wrote a book, The Seven Spiritual Laws of Success. I feel that law number two, the Law of Giving, helps describe my theory; the more I share, the more I win. Statistically, the opposite should be true. The more people that enter a sweepstakes should decrease my odds of winning. However, I believe the opposite to be true, "I can't lose helping others win".

I share/post as many sweepstakes, answers, and help as often as I can to as many groups as I can. I know there are people within those groups entering many more sweepstakes than I do. Yet, since 2004 I consistently win 100+ prizes each year. Why do I win 5, 10, 15+ sweepstakes every month (month after month)? Why have I not paid for a vacation in years? I believe it directly ties into the Law of Giving.

> That is why you must give and receive in order to keep wealth and affluence—or anything you want in life—circulating in your life.

> The word affluence comes from the root word "affluere," which means "to flow to." The word affluence means "to flow in abundance." Money is really a symbol of the life energy we exchange and the life energy we use as a result of the service we provide to the universe. Another word for money is "currency," which also reflects the flowing nature of energy. The word currency comes from the Latin word "currere" which means "to run" or to flow.

> Therefore, if we stop the circulation of money—if our only intention is to hold on to our money and hoard it—since it is life energy, we will stop its circulation back into our lives as well. In order to keep that energy coming to us, we have to keep the energy circulating. Like a river, money must keep flowing, otherwise it begins to stagnate, to clog, to suffocate and strangle its very own life force. Circulation keeps it alive and vital.

> Every relationship is one of give and take. Giving engenders receiving, and receiving engenders giving. What goes up must come down; what goes out must come back. In reality, receiving is the same thing as giving, because giving and receiving are different aspects of the flow of energy in the universe. And if you stop the flow of either, you interfere with nature's intelligence.

> The more you give, the more you will receive, because you will keep the abundance of the universe circulating in your life. In fact, anything that is of value in life only multiplies when it is given. That which doesn't multiply through giving is neither worth giving nor worth receiving. If, through the act of giving, you feel you have lost something, then the gift is not truly given

and will not cause increase. If you give grudgingly, there is no energy behind that giving.

It is the intention behind your giving and receiving that is the most important thing. The intention should always be to create happiness for the giver and receiver, because happiness is life-supporting and life-sustaining and therefore generates increase. The return is directly proportional to the giving when it is unconditional and from the heart. That is why the act of giving has to be joyful—the frame of mind has to be one in which you feel joy in the very act of giving. Then the energy behind the giving increases many times over.

Practicing the Law of Giving is actually very simple: if you want joy, give joy to others; if you want love, learn to give love; if you want attention and appreciation, learn to give attention and appreciation; if you want material affluence, help others to become materially affluent. In fact, the easiest way to get what you want is to help others get what they want. This principle works equally well for individuals, corporations, societies, and nations. If you want to be blessed with all the good things in life learn to silently bless everyone with all the good things in life.

From the book The Seven Spiritual Laws of Success © 1994, Deepak Chopra. Reprinted by permission of Amber-Allen Publishing, Inc. P.O. Box 6657, San Rafael, CA 94903. All rights reserved.

"Every action generates a force of energy that returns to us in like kind...what we sow is what we reap.
And when we choose actions that bring happiness and success to others, the fruit of our karma is happiness and success."
Deepak Chopra

Good Karma

Galatians 6:7 Do not be deceived. God will not be made a fool. **For a person will reap what he sows,** 6:8 because the person who sows to his own flesh will reap corruption from the flesh, but the one who sows to the Spirit will reap eternal life from the Spirit.

The bible states you reap what you sow. You sow good fortune for others; you reap good fortune for yourself. This also ties back into the Law of Attraction—like attracting like.

I believe the expression "cheaters never win." You may cheat, and you may win that particular sweepstakes, but you will lose somewhere else in your life. It is not worth cheating.

Gary Zukav spoke eloquently in his book Soul Stories about how the cycle of getting what you give ties us with the Universe.

> Another gift that you get from the Universe is an experience that is perfect for you. This gift comes each moment from the time you were born until you die.
>
> You and the Universe create this gift together. You decide what it will be, and the Universe gives it to you. That is the Golden Rule—what you do to people, people do to you. It is also called karma. If you don't like what people do to you, you can change that by doing things different to them. That is how you and the Universe work together. Each moment you choose a new gift, and, when the time is right, the Universe gives it to you.
>
> Each day brings gifts that you have ordered, and each day you place more orders. You do this by setting you intentions, and then acting on them. The Universe takes your orders, and delivers them. Everyone gets what she or he ordered. If you order fear, you get it. If you order love, you get it.
>
> When you order, you share with the Universe. When your order is filled, the Universe shares with you. Complaining about your gifts is walking in the fog. Recognizing your gifts—and who ordered them—is walking in the sunshine.
>
> Walking in the sunshine is clarity.

Reprinted with the permission of Simon & Schuster Adult Publishing Group from SOUL STORIES by Gary Zukav. Copyright © 2000 by Gary Zukav

RESOURCE: Robert Ohotto is the author of Transforming Fate into Destiny and host of an online radio show called Soul Connexions. www.ohotto.com.

Help Stop Cheating

It's also good karma to help stop any cheating you come across. Companies spend hundreds, thousands and sometimes tens of thousands of dollars running contests. They do not want their marketing efforts sabotaged. They want to hear from you as they want their prospects and customers to have a positive experience with their company. If possible, they will do everything in their power to disqualify cheaters and award prizes properly.

Sadly, there are bloggers, agencies and sponsors that just don't care, and your efforts will seem wasted as the cheaters win. I recommend you always take the high road continuing to communicate your concerns as incidents occur. As nothing is permanent; companies merge, staff changes and the playing field shifts, your next communication may be acted upon.

The fastest way to communicate your concerns is via social media. I recommend Facebook and Twitter. If you do not get a positive response, your next course of action would be to find out who the Vice President of Marketing is of the contest sponsor and mail them a letter. (Yes, a paper letter sent via snail mail as emails can be ignored, but paper mail isn't ignored any longer.)

Always express your concerns in a positive manner. Whining and complaining will not get your grievance taken as seriously as one that is geared to elevate the sponsor out of a potential public relations fiasco.

"Gratitude is one of the easiest and most powerful ways to transform your life. If you become truly grateful, you will magnetize absolute joy to you everywhere you go, and in everything you do."
Rhonda Byrnes

STORY: It is important to thank the sponsors when you win. Gratitude and karma go hand-in-hand.

∩∪

Terry—Fairport, NY
It is important to always thank the sponsors when you win. For smaller wins I usually go to the sponsor's website and use their "Contact Us" feature to email a thank you. For larger wins, I send a hand-written thank you note.

∩∪

"The Universe rewards action."
Jack Canfield

Just do it!

I enter almost every sweepstakes I come across. (I would enter more except I do not have the time.) In sales it is called a numbers game. The more prospects you call on, the more sales you are going to make. Similarly, I believe the more sweepstakes I enter, the more sweepstakes I am going to win.

Making Your Own Luck

Lynne's luck started when she happened to come across a newspaper article describing how a woman had won several impressive competition prizes. Lynne therefore decided to enter a crossword competition and won £10. A few weeks later she entered another competition and won three sports bikes. Shortly afterwards, she went to an interview for a position teaching an evening class in fashion design. There was a coffee jar on the interviewer's desk and it had a competition entry form on it. Lynne was drawn to this and asked if she could have the label. The interviewer asked why she wanted it and Lynne told her about how she had won some competitions. The interviewer asked her to come teach two evening classes—one on fashion design and one on how to win competitions. Lynne accepted the offer and also started to enter lots more competitions. Her winning streak continued and she won lots more prizes, including two cars and several holidays abroad.

Interestingly, these competition wins allowed Lynne to achieve her lifelong ambition of becoming a freelance writer. In 1992 she wrote a book on winning competitions. To publicize the book, a press release was sent to her local paper and they published an article about her work. The next day, the story was picked up by the national newspapers and she was invited to appear on several television shows. As a result, Lynne was invited to write newspaper articles on winning competitions. In 1996 she received a telephone call from a major daily newspaper. They had seen her work and asked her to write a daily competition column for them. Her column, 'Win with Lynne', was highly successful and ran for many years.

Lynne has fulfilled many of her lifelong ambitions, been happily married for over forty years and has a wonderful family life. Like many people involved in my research, Lynne attributes much of her success to good fortune.

Wendy is a 40-year-old housewife. She considers herself lucky in many aspects of her life, but is especially fortunate when it comes to winning competitions. On average, she wins about three prizes a week. Some of these prizes are quite small, but many have been substantial. In the last five years she has won large cash prizes and several major holidays abroad. Wendy certainly seems to have a magical ability to win competitions—and she is not the only one. In the previous chapter I described how Lynne has won several large prizes in competitions, including several cars and holidays.

The same is also true of Joe. Like both Wendy and Lynne, Joe considers himself to be very lucky in many areas of his life. He has been happily married for forty years and has a loving family. However, Joe is especially lucky in competitions, and his recent successes include winning televisions, a day spent on the set of a well-known television soap opera, and several holidays.

What is behind Lynne, Wendy and Joe's winning ways? Their secret is surprisingly simple. They all enter a very large number of competitions.

Each week, Wendy enters about sixty postal competitions, and about seventy Internet-based competitions. Likewise, both Lynne and Joe enter about fifty competitions a week, and their chances of winning are increased with each and every entry. All three of them were well aware that their lucky winning ways are, in reality, due to the large number of competitions they enter. As Wendy explained, 'I am a lucky person, but luck is what you make it. I win a lot of competitions and prizes, but I do put a huge amount of effort into it.'

Joe commented: People always said to me they think I'm very lucky because of the amount of competitions that I win. But then they tell me that they don't enter many themselves, and I think, "Well, if you don't enter, you have no chance of winning." They look at me as being very lucky, but I think you make your own luck ... as I say to them 'You've got to be in to win.'

From THE LUCK FACTOR by Dr. Richard Wiseman. Copyright © 2003 Dr. Richard Wiseman. By permission of

"You inner world, the mental, the emotional and the spiritual, creates your outer world, the physical."
T. Harv Eker

"Winning is important to me, but what brings me real joy is the experience of being fully engaged in whatever I'm doing."
Phil Jackson

CONCLUSION

If you were new to sweeping when you began reading this book I hope I have turned you into a savvy sweeper. If you were a seasoned sweeper, I hope I have helped you learn a few tips, tricks and about the new technologies. My goal when I began writing this book was to teach people about the hobby of sweeping and hopefully, have as much fun as I do dreaming, entering and winning.

STORY: Lynn was a very wonderful woman who was as passionate about sweeping as I am. Sadly, Lynn passed away in 2005 and I never had the opportunity to meet her in person. I wanted to share with you her luckiest day. May we all be as lucky as Lynn one day.

෨෬

One of the most exciting days of my life was the day I started getting dressed to go and pick-up the car I had won. My husband called and while we were talking the "call waiting beep" warned me another call was on the line. It was a judging agency asking me to answer a skill testing question. I answered correctly so they informed me I won a trip to Greece. Ken was still on hold so I excitedly told him about my latest win. As we were talking the mail man arrived with a registered letter informing me I had won a trip to Mexico! You can imagine Ken's surprise when I told him I just won a second trip to Mexico. A car and two trips all in one day! I'm still working on topping that one.

Extract from WINNING WAYS by Lynn Banks Goutbeck and Melanie Rockett. Used by permission of Proof Positive Productions Ltd. www.proofpositive.com

෨෬

RESOURCE: Melanie Rockett rereleased her 2nd book The Contest Guru's Guide To Winning www.contestguru.com.

Remember, **you can't win if you don't enter.**

ACKNOWLEDGEMENTS

I am truly grateful for all those who helped me write this book and make it a success.

Gwen Beauchamp, Scott Bourgeois, Bill Carey, Ken and Diane Carlos, Jennifer Day, Marc Gagnon, Sylvia Gold, Jeff Goodfield, Greg Goodson, Sandra Grauschopf, Parry Grubb, Joe Head, Evert Hoff, Linda Horricks, David Larade, Wendy Limague, Craig McDaniel, Ron Miller, Dana Noga, Lori Novak, Patti Osterheld, Donna Ralph, Brent Riley, Melanie Rockett, Allen Sayward, Todd Schwartzfarb, Dan and Mike Skeen, Sacha Sylvain, Nick Taylor, Kate Thompson, Karen Weix.

To all the sweepstakes club members because they taught me that friendship is the best prize of this hobby: Paula A., Sharon A., Vicki A., Cecilia B., Linda-Jo B., Tena B., Diane C., Denise C., Karla D., Marge D., Steve D., Becky E., Denise F., Paula F., Ret F., Steve F., BJ G., Deb H., Mary Ann H., Sheryl H., Ingrid J., Mike and Julie J., Mary K., Nancy K., Patty K., Maureen Kennerk, Barbara L., Arlene M., Brenda M., Diane M., John M., Joy M., Judy M., Linda M., Pam M., Maria Miller, Laura O., Harmony P., Julian P., Paula P., Wendy P., Rita S., Terry S., Joyce T., Sue T., Gail W.

To all those who regaled me with wonderful, and often funny, stories of their sweepstaking adventures: Al-Dearborn MI, Bea-Toronto ON, Carmen-Norfolk VA, Evelyn-Queen Anne MD, Fred-Prince George BC, Joe-Warren MI, Lynn-Whitby ON, Mary-St. Albert AB, Melanie-Repentigny, QC, Rachel-Morrisville NC, Rick-Pickering ON, Sharon-Aurora ON, Susan-Rose Bay NS, Tamara-Syracuse NY, Terry-Fairport NY, Tina-Wapakoneta OH, Tracy-Burke VA, Vickie-Dallas OR.

To all my editors who keep my spelling, grammar and writing on track: Jason Block, Tom Cavalli, Carol McLaughlin, David Osborne, and my mom Louisa Sislian.

And finally, Stephanie Wells who helped me rewrite the Play Safe chapter.

Manufactured by Amazon.ca
Bolton, ON